T0284885

THE MOST INTERESTING MAN IN THE WORLD

THE MOST INTERESTING MAN IN THE WORLD

VINNIE STIGMA
WITH HOWIE ABRAMS

PERMUTED
PRESS

A PERMUTED PRESS BOOK

The Most Interesting Man in the World
© 2024 by Vinnie Stigma with Howie Abrams
All Rights Reserved

ISBN: 978-1-63758-465-1
ISBN (eBook): 978-1-63758-466-8

Cover art by Donna McLeer / Tunnel Vizion Media, LLC
Interior design and composition, Greg Johnson, Textbook Perfect
Front cover image by Heather McGrath
Back cover image by Maurice Del-Ciotto

PERMUTED
PRESS

Permuted Press, LLC
New York • Nashville
permutedpress.com

Published in the United States of America
1 2 3 4 5 6 7 8 9 10

Dedicated to my family, friends,
Agnostic Front members past and present,
and all those we've lost along the way.

Howie dedicates this book to Julie and Nia
for everything you are and do.

"*Impossible is just a big word thrown around by small men who find it easier to live in the world they've been given than to explore the power they have to change it. Impossible is not a fact. It's an opinion. Impossible is not a declaration. It's a dare. Impossible is potential. Impossible is temporary. Impossible is nothing.*"

—MUHAMMAD ALI

Contents

Foreword

By Roger Miret

"Vinnie is going to outlive everybody. He's going to be the last person standing. If a nuclear bomb goes off, only roaches and Stigma will live. That's it."

Vinnie Stigma and I connected pretty much right away. He says he was dancing beside me at a show—I believe it was at the Peppermint Lounge—and liked my style in the pit. That's where I had my first sort of encounter with him. I'd been watching him on the dance floor, and he would go against the grain, or just stand in the middle of everyone. You could tell he was a character right away just from watching him. We hadn't spoken a word to one another yet; that was at some random CBGB show soon afterward. And I don't think our conversation had anything to do with music or punk rock. I'm pretty sure he was in the midst of a conversation with someone, comparing who made the best meatballs or something ridiculous like that. He's Italian, so...you know, a natural mamaluke.

Vinnie was really easy to approach, especially for that time, when everyone was kinda crazy. You didn't feel intimidated to speak to him or anything like that. He was friendly to everyone, as opposed to some other people on the scene who seemed like they had to get a little bit more comfortable with you first. He's never been arrogant either, even though he probably had the right to be. Vinnie has never been like that, and he's still not. He's a very easy creature, a creature of habit. When he is hungry, he eats, when he is tired, he sleeps, but in the end, playing the show is always the biggest thing in the world to him. It doesn't matter how you're feeling, or what mood you're in; for Vinnie, you have to forget about that, play your show, and entertain those who've paid to see you. We've both played shows while sick as dogs. He's always like, "We have to play. The show must go on." That time at CBGB when he split his head open, I was at the hospital with him while the show was still going on, and he told me, "No, you have to go back and play. We can't disappoint anyone." Early on, I recognized that attitude in him, and I know that's what he believes when it comes to Agnostic Front. We share that attitude and so many other things.

As far as winding up in a band together, things didn't start to happen until one night at Great Gildersleeves, where I think the Angry Samoans were playing. I was in the pit doing my thing; stage diving, and just being a regular New York hardcore dancer or whatever. Vinnie and I had become friends by then, and that day, he had Adam (Mucci) and Raybeez approach me to join their band. I was a little bit confused, because, first of all, I wasn't a straight-up vocalist. I always played bass and did a little bit of vocals in The Psychos. "Are you looking for a bass player?" Adam was already the bass player, so it was weird. They told me they wanted me to sing. I guess Stigma saw me going crazy on the dance floor and figured that's what he needed me to do. Back then, as long as you looked good going crazy, that was enough. That's how it used to be—no experience necessary. I don't even think he asked me to try out, he just told me, "I really want you to be in the band." He knew I was already with The Psychos, but at that time, people were always in multiple bands. It didn't matter because we were all in it for the scene, so it wasn't like, "Oh, you're stealing somebody from my band." Nobody thought about touring, nobody ever thought about anything more than just having fun and playing some songs, that's it.

We eventually got together and started to rehearse at this little dungeon down by Vinnie, somewhere in NoHo. We would close the door and it would be steaming hot. Raybeez would be wearing seven layers of clothes. By the time we were done, he was down to just his underwear. We were doing songs that we each already had and brought to the group. We'd all gravitated toward this American skinhead thing. That was our style. That's what Negative Approach was doing and what SSD was doing and what Minor Threat was doing. It wasn't like the UK skinhead look; it was more our own thing. We didn't have Dr. Martens. You had to mail order those from England back then. Who had the money to do that? I still have my zipper combat boots; that's what we wore. But then, being that we were in New York, it became edgier. At the time, we were more punk rock. We still had mohawks and spiked hair and stuff like that, but the scene was changing over to the American hardcore vibe those bands were doing. The whole skinhead thing was about trying to disassociate ourselves from the traditional punks that were like, "Fuck the world, fuck everything, live fast, die young...." We—not just Agnostic Front, but SSD, Minor Threat, Negative Approach—were all moving to disassociate from that and create our own thing. We were definitely, "Fuck this, fuck that," but it was not about destroying everything. It was more like, "Let's make a difference. Let's make a change." We were the younger generation. Later on, we even disassociated ourselves from what we became. The UK skinhead thing became really heavy, and we needed to separate ourselves from that also. You know the lyrics: "United and strong, blacks and white, punks and skins." That's where we were coming from.

Vinnie played guitar. He actually used to be the bass player with The Eliminators, and then he switched to guitar. He had all the gear too: everything for everybody. Nobody else owned anything. He had bass gear, then he decided to get his guitar and an amp. He bought the drums.... We would just take it all to CBGB to play, then back again. Vinnie's drum kit was the house drum kit at CBs for the longest, A7 too.

As far as Vinnie's playing style as a guitarist, it was great. There wasn't, and still isn't, anyone like him. He had this unique way of playing.

I mean, if you notice, a lot of songs on *United Blood* and *Victim in Pain* are completely out of tune. If you were to ask Don Fury, he'd tell you that he had the hardest time trying to keep Vinnie's guitar in tune. It wasn't the guitar, it was the way Vinnie plays. He grabs those strings and bends the shit out of them! His pinkie is always floating behind the fretboard. He's also pressing his thumb through the fretboard on the backside, and all the other fingers, minus his pinkie, are counterpressuring from the other side. It's wild. But back then, people didn't really care about how great a musician anyone was. Agnostic Front was not a great band musically. We were like watching a controlled train wreck. It was about the show, and we got that from Stigma. You had to watch what was going on. It was theatrical more than anything. We were a laughingstock as far as musicianship, but in the end, we prevailed over all of the other early NYHC bands because we were genuine. We were real people doing real things. It wasn't about the best technical playing, or politics, or any of this other bullshit. It was just about, "Hey, you want to see a real fucking band? This is real hardcore. These guys are nuts. They're jumping on you, they're doing all this stuff, and they're barely playing the fucking song."

A funny story about our song "Power" from *Victim in Pain*: It was introduced to us by Vinnie right before we recorded that album. It had originally been an Eliminators song, and we loved it. It was a bit odd for us because we were more classic American hardcore punk, and "Power" was our version of an Oi! kind of thing. I don't know what possessed me to yell "*Stigma*" just before the lead Vinnie plays. I created a fucking monster with that. I created my own Eddie from Iron Maiden just by yelling "Stigma" during that song. Seriously, it was just me having fun and being a jerk, just like, "Stigma, my guitar hero!" It kinda turned him into one.

Around the time of *Victim in Pain*, I can remember the day I felt like Vinnie and I were finally making an impact with the band. It was a show we played at the Jane Street Rock Hotel with Kraut. We went on before them, and the place went nuts! Then Kraut went on and it seemed like nobody cared. It was really weird too because I always loved Kraut, but this time, it was about us. Then, the next time we played a show at CBGB—the first time with *Victim in Pain* out—I'd never seen CBs so full. People came from all over. We were already kind of a local favorite in New York City, but then, all of a sudden, people showed up from beyond our friend group at A7. People had really come to see us from places like Jersey, Connecticut, Pennsylvania…. I remember thinking, *Maybe we're doing something good here. Maybe we're on to something.*

Fast-forward all these years, and I think the bond between me and Vinnie has lasted for good reason. Other guys who've been in Agnostic Front always wound up having different things going on in their lives. Some started having kids, or they just moved on. I did the same thing, but I had my first kid and never moved on. Vinnie and I have always been passionate about this thing. Our friendship is very passionate, and we love our band. It means a lot to us, and we still enjoy what we do. It's genuine love and true sincerity. That's what has kept us together as friends all these years, and also as a band. We simply love what we do and want to keep doing it.

For a long time, I was living in abandoned buildings or in a van and often in Vinnie's apartment during the harsh, cold winters. That's where I had my showers, where I escaped the more difficult times. Vinnie had the headquarters. He had 285 Mott Street, and he had the phone. We organized everything for the band there. We assembled the *United Blood* single there. All the band mail would come to Vinnie's. We needed a stable place, and Vinnie had that stable place for people to know how to contact us. He had our gear there too. We created this tight relationship that worked for both of us. We never argued about anything; religion was never anything for us, money was never anything. It's all been trust and love.

I'll never forget when I picked him up in the van to leave for one of our first tours, right after he quit his job. He had literally just finished beating the shit out of his foreman. He was dying to beat that guy up.

I think he hit him with a fucking two-by-four. He was just looking for that moment for us to hit the road.

Vinnie is like family, still is and always will be. My mother considers Vinnie family, my brothers consider Vinnie family, my sister…I mean, all of them talk to him constantly, texting each other and all that. Vinnie has no brothers or sisters. I am his brother. He has no other living person as close to him as I am.

Think about the situation with my brother Freddy, when Vinnie basically had to become his guardian for a while. Imagine, Freddy's a teenager, and I needed to leave him—my younger brother—at Vinnie's place to live and be in his care. Amy and I didn't have a great living situation together with Freddy, so he needed to leave. Vinnie welcomed him in. He needed to be going to school, so Vinnie was like, "Don't worry about it, Roger, I got this." He'd call my mom and check in all the time. That's how it was. That's a whole different level of friendship and trust and love. He helped raise my brother. Vinnie wasn't always the most responsible person, but he became extremely responsible when it came to Freddy. He knew he couldn't fuck that up.

Stigma's always been a strange creature. He will purposely sabotage something so that he never has to do it again. For example, driving: he almost fucking drove the band off a cliff, so we never asked him to drive again. He did shit like that purposely. With interviews, ask him whatever you want, but he's probably just going to talk about the Pittsburgh Steelers. He has a way of doing stuff like that. I remember when he and his mom would get into these crazy arguments. He just would not do what she asked, and she'd never ask him again. He's no dummy. Thankfully, with Freddy, the last thing he wanted to do was fuck anything up with my mom or my brothers or me. That's how much respect he's always had for us. Vinnie loves his sleep, but he'd get up with Freddy every morning and tell him, "You gotta go to school." Freddy never wanted to go, but Vinnie would be like, "Goddammit, you gotta go to school!" People talk about bonds of friendship and all this stuff, but talk is just talk.

That's something real about Agnostic Front—and me and Vinnie. We've
always walked the walk. We've lived it.

Our foundation is as strong as it could ever be. It's been knocked
down a few times, and it's been a wild roller-coaster ride with way-ups
and way-downs. It still goes up and down. And I learned from Vinnie
that you better be nice to people, because you're going to see the same
people on the way up that you see on the way down. If you were a jackass
on the way up, and now things aren't going so well, they're gonna be up
there laughing at you. Together, we've enjoyed every bit of the ups and
downs and have enjoyed everywhere we've gone.

Every time we go to a different country, we want to eat what the local
people eat. For instance, we've had guys in the band, and still do, who are
like, "Oh, I don't eat Japanese food." I mean, we're in fucking Japan! Or
we're in Mexico; "I don't eat Mexican food." Just eat what the people eat,
because we come from a background where, for a while, there was nothing. In the beginning, the meal we ate religiously, three times a day, was
two hot dogs and a Coke from 7-Eleven. Why? Because we only had five
dollars a day to eat. It's crazy to think that now, at many of the festival
shows we play overseas, there are actual chefs who cook for us.

Touring the world several times over with Vinnie has been super easy.
It's one thing to be in a local band where you go home and sleep in your
own bed after a show. It's a whole different animal to take the show on
the road. You learn quickly who's tour-worthy and who's not. I've worked
with some great people: great musicians, great friends, but you can't take
a lot of them on tour. Vinnie is easygoing. I honestly don't remember any
complaints from that guy. We've always moved as a unit. I don't necessarily think of our adventures as if I've been seeing the world with, say, my
wife, or something like that, but it's actually been kind of like that. It's
sort of like here we are as a family, and we're doing this together. Doing
all of this with Stigma has been very special. We never believed we'd do
anything like this. I mean, I didn't know there was anything beyond New
York City. I didn't even know there was a Buffalo, New York, let alone

having the opportunity to see all of the US, or Europe, or Asia, or South America. Back then, Stigma and I probably would've laughed in your face if you told us what we'd do. People start bands now, and they expect to get an instant fan base because of the internet. They've never had to be in a van or deal with what comes along with that. They don't know what it's like to have to build something from the ground up. All these years later, nobody knows how to do it better than me and Vinnie.

He's just a great person, and there's never a dull moment with this man. Shit, I looked on the internet the other day, and he was actually wrestling at a real wrestling event. Wrestling! I mean, he just celebrates his life. There's no ill will in Vinnie Stigma; there's nothing mean. If you cross him, he could have issues with you, but he's a genuinely happy person and lives his life by happy means. He doesn't want any confrontation. He hates it. He wants no schism. He wants everybody to be happy, he wants everybody to get along. He doesn't understand the seriousness of situations sometimes, and we have to let him know, "Vinnie, this is serious." To him, it's almost never serious. He just genuinely wants to live his life to its fullest. I've never met anybody who lives like Vinnie; never a worry or concern, it's amazing. We joke about it, but it's the truth: Vinnie Stigma really is the most interesting man in the world, and there's no better entertainer out there than him.

Introduction

IF I HAD A DOLLAR FOR EVERY instance in which someone said to me, "The first time I went to a CBGB hardcore matinee, I met Vinnie Stigma," I'd likely top *Forbes*'s list of wealthiest Americans. In fact, during my own virgin voyage to 315 Bowery on a Sunday afternoon in 1984, Vinnie served as an unofficial welcoming committee. As I loitered alone in front of the legendary venue between bands at a show headlined by New Jersey's Adrenalin O.D., mere feet from the joint's decrepit front doors, Vin approached me, asking in his unmistakable New-Yo-talian dialect, "Hey! You here to see the show?" He must have seen the met-alhead-transitioning-to-hardcore-kid written all over me. I probably responded chock full of corniness, exclaiming, "Fuck yeah," or something like that. He chirped back with, "Good! Glad you came. See you inside." I knew who he was, but was shocked that he was speaking to me. Count-less others recall similar encounters with this icon; presenting as a New York City–style skinhead, complete with neck tattoo—the first I'd ever seen in person—openly welcoming one and all complete strangers into his universe. An environment which would quickly become ours too for decades to come, in no small part thanks to Vinnie Stigma.

Vinnie is rightfully recognized as one of NYC hardcore's elder statesmen. He is Agnostic Front's founder and guitarist, in addition to being one of the Big Apple's earliest punk rockers. There are few more beloved and respected figures in the history of the city that never sleeps than this man. He made his bones on Mott Street in Little Italy among the tight-knit immigrant families, and even a few of the wise guys who resided among them. To call Vinnie a character understates the obvious. Born Vincent Capuccio on December 3, 1955, "Stigma," as his countless friends and fans lovingly refer to him, has glided through his almost seven decades on earth as youthfully and purposefully as anyone ever has. To many, he is the everyman, yet to others, he is a superhero. His thick accent is charming as hell, and his manner is every bit as inviting. He is someone who respects and loves tradition, yet wholeheartedly embraces progress. Vinnie is your paesan, and you are his. Whether onstage armed with his trusty Gibson SG, or sharing a bowl of lovingly prepared ravioli with a guest in his home, there's nowhere you'd rather be than in his presence.

On stage, Stigma is simply unlike any performer you've ever laid eyes on. He displays little regard for anything other than entertaining those before him, even if it means removing his instrument mid-song to mosh with the "kids" as he affectionately calls them. This is Vinnie's modus operandi; to entertain no matter the platform or the conditions. Most charmingly, Stigma applies the same MO to his conversations with friends, family, and fans: not dissimilarly to your favorite uncle or grandparent before whom the brood gathers at each and every holiday celebration, so as to embrace grand, colorful tales of yesteryear and magnificently imparted wisdom. Each nugget dispensed in a manner only such a charmingly idiosyncratic voice as Vinnie's can do justice to.

Pull up a seat and sponge a few anecdotes about old New York, or maybe the birth of punk rock, or his love for Frank Sinatra, Jimi Hendrix, and Bruce Lee, or the story about how he cheated death while getting his first tattoo in Harlem. He might let you in on how the downtown mafioso coexisted with the other immigrants in his beloved Little Italy when he was growing up. Of course he'll discuss his life as an international touring musician, and all the places and amazing things he's experienced.

No one sees or describes the world quite like Vinnie Stigma. You are soon to cherish these tales, as I and so many others have. Whether you are a hardcore OG, new jack, or somewhere in between, this gem of a human being is—if he hasn't already—going to occupy a little bit of emotional real estate within you.

—*Howie Abrams*

Prologue

I WAS LUCKY TO BE BORN in New York City. I'm a second-generation American and New Yorker. My grandparents on one side came from Italy, and the other side was born here. The Italian side came in the late 1890s before the real big wave. My father was born across the street from the church at 209 Mott Street, right on his family's kitchen table, and I was born in Saint Clare's Hospital in Hell's Kitchen. They don't even call it "Hell's Kitchen" anymore, they call it "Clinton" now. It's all a real estate ploy: DUMBO, NoLIta…. They've been taking the heart out of my city for a long time now. Fucking Mayor Giuliani, then Bloomberg…. You can't smoke. You can't drink. They don't want you to have soda. You can't park anywhere because of the bike lanes. And there are so few true New Yorkers left. When I'm walking behind people on the street, I'm like, "Come on, move it along, walk the right way! At least pretend you're from here." They're like, "But I live here." Yeah, you may live here now, but you're not *from* here. You moved here from somewhere else. I can tell by how you walk.

Here in Little Italy, when the Italians first came over, all the "Neapol-dons" (Neapolitans) lived on Mott Street, and all the Sicilians, like Marty Scorsese, lived on Elizabeth Street. His mother and my mother used to go to the church right down here. Back then, the Italians had to go down to the basement of the church for mass, because the church was run by "other people," but that's another story. Way before they had the famous San Gennaro feast, it was called the San Rocco feast. Remember in *The Godfather* when the old Mustache Pete pinned the hundred-dollar bill on the saint? That was on Saint Rocco, who was also my saint. That was the old mafioso in Little Italy. I'd walk out my door and boom, there they were across the street. They used to wear the long coats because they were carrying machine guns. Joe Action, Cheech, all the guys. They had the club, Murder Inc., Lefty's club, which was associated with another club right over here.

One of the guys had a pigeon coop over on the next roof from me, and when I was a kid, I used to go over and take care of his pigeons. They'd pluck all the feathers so they couldn't fly away because they were fancy and expensive. He had like seven hundred of them in three different coops, totally trained. The whole pigeon-coop-on-the-roof thing is an old Italian tradition. I loved it and threw myself into it because I knew it would disappear one day. It was my way of attaching myself to old New York and these great traditions. I remember my grandfather not changing out of the dirty shirt he'd wear around the pigeons. The whole pigeon thing was dirty, but believe me, if the internet goes down, you'll be relying on these guys with pigeons to communicate.

Music really became a thing for me when I listened to an old Enrico Caruso record my family had. He was an opera singer from the same town in Italy my grandmother came from. When I heard this thing, with all the pops and scratches because it was such an old record, it sounded so authentic and was so powerful and overwhelm-  ing to me. I was like, "*Wow*, this guy's so cool and so great." Then, in the '60s, of course, I heard The Beatles, but I also heard Frank Sinatra. I always liked Frank because I thought he was the coolest guy there was. He could probably have killed someone and gotten away with it. But then…I heard Jimi Hendrix. It was Hendrix who really did it for me. Around the same time, Bruce Lee had a big influence on me. Bruce was a tough guy, which I admired, and I tried to represent myself like, "I'm a tough guy too." I grew up very close to Chinatown, so everyone over here knew about Bruce Lee before the rest of America saw him in the movies. I wanted to be like both of those guys: Jimi Hendrix and Bruce Lee—the toughest man on earth and the greatest guitar player who ever lived. Jimi liberated the guitar, and I don't think there'd be any of this MMA stuff going on now if it wasn't for Bruce. He exposed everyone in the country to martial arts. He turned it into sports entertainment. It's why I tell the guys in Agnostic Front when we play shows: we're here to play, but really, we're here to entertain people.

I got a lot deeper into music around the time of the British Invasion, plus all the rock and glam rock that was happening. There were lots of great groups and great songs. Then I heard all the Detroit stuff like MC5 and The Stooges. There was a lot of music happening in the early to mid-'70s. Here in New York, we had the New York Dolls, Dead Boys, The Dictators…. I lived, and still live, around the corner from CBGB. You can hit it with a snowball from my house. I went to clubs like Max's Kansas City and Great Gildersleeves. There was this guy, Johnny Saponaro, who's dead now. He was my mentor as far as playing music. Great guy, smart guy. Went to Xavier High School. He taught us all how to play, and we started this band called Black Angus. Another guy was Angelo Bird, but he got run out of the neighborhood. Around '77, '78, I had a band called The Eliminators, which was a good time but it eventually ran its course. Then, around '82 I started what I called Zoo Crew, which was us just fucking around playing hardcore punk. I mean, I was never gonna stay in a band called "Zoo Crew," you know what I mean?! Then, there was Agnostic Front. I would never have thought we'd still be doing it this many years later—and maybe better than ever.

Man, we've had a lot of members in and out of Agnostic Front—a lot of great guys and musicians. I don't really know why the lineup has changed so many times. Maybe it's all the transitions and the way we jumped around with our sound. Plus, van touring is hard, especially for as long as we've been doing it. Some people aren't built for it and just can't hang. You know, you're in a band with somebody; it's great for a weekend. But you go on tour for two months, and you want to choke them to death! All of us in a van, packed with gear, and a dog, a raccoon, a cow.... We tried to get a billy goat in there once but it squirmed too much.

Bottom line: I always feel grateful for what I've got, and that's the end of that. I would never want someone, anywhere, who I don't even know, to say, "Vinnie Stigma: he's a real rock star asshole." I would never want that. I would never want to be perceived that way. There's always gonna be a band bigger than your band, and there's gonna be a band bigger than that band. I don't do this for that reason, to be big and popular. I do this to have a platform. I do it to send a message, or to unite kids, or to inspire kids to maybe get in a band, or play an instrument. Maybe you play guitar and you never get to be a rock star, but you play an instrument, and you can pass that on to somebody. Life ain't about tweeting to see how many likes you get, that much I know.

mensch noun

\ 'men(t)sh \

Definition of *mensch*
: a person of integrity and honor

1

"Stigma"

Everybody back in the old school punk rock days had a nickname: "Johnny Thunders," "Sid Vicious," "Iggy Pop," "Billy Psycho…." Even The Ramones were all "Ramones." During the Max's Kansas City days, I picked "Stigma." I figured I wanted to make sure the name was believable, so I picked what sounded like an Italian name. It's really just a nickname, but everyone caught on and started calling me "Stigma," so I was like, "Okay, 'Stigma' it is."

2

Son

My father was a first-generation American. He was a truck driver and also drove for Lenny Riggio, who owned Barnes & Noble. Lenny's father was boxer Steve Riggio, who actually fought Rocky Graziano twice in one month. My dad was a regular neighborhood guy who loved Cadillacs and drove other guys around. Back in the day, they would call that a "wheel man." He was a good guy: a typical smoker, drinker, and a  gambler. His nickname was "Sonny Beef," even though his real name was Vincent (I am Vincent Junior, and my son is Vincent III).

Due to the fact that my mom, Teresa, had me later in life—at thirty-two, which was old for that era—I am an only child. My mother was sickly as a young adult due to tuberculosis and had only one lung. Up until she broke her hip, she was the chef at St. Anthony's Church on Houston Street. She served bishops and cardinals who all loved her cooking because she made all the old school dishes. When she suffered her hip injury, she couldn't make it to the church, so the priest would come up to the house and give her communion. I remember seeing Monsignor Marinacci in my kitchen having coffee with my mother. I used to play at the church when I was a kid. It was nice and cool there in the summertime. My dad and uncles would hang out there too. On Sundays, all the men would gather down there to talk and drink.

In 1925, a brand new building opened here at 285 Mott Street and my parents moved in. They even got married there. They had their wedding party on the roof—and had to use a few other roofs too. Using other roofs is how all those people were able to be at the wedding. There were so many people on different roofs that they called it a "football wedding," because everyone would throw their sandwiches from one roof to another.

The apartment I am in right now was once occupied by Vincent Coll, who worked for The Outfit in Chicago, and basically invented the drive-by (shooting). He was with Murder Incorporated. After Vincent, the next occupant was a veteran, and then my aunt moved into it. It was empty for a while, but my family held onto it until I moved in in 1975. All of my father's family lived in this building at one point. My grandmother lived across the hall in B18, a few doors from me. I remember my grandparents living here and hearing stories of my grandfather having a wine cellar downstairs in 1927 when there was still prohibition. My grandfather was the wine guy in the neighborhood. When my grandfather passed away, my grandmother wore a veil and dressed in black all the time. Her shoes looked like those black Christopher Columbus shoes. The whole mourning process involved no TV and no radio. It went on for at least a year, if not two. Very old-country kind of stuff.

When I was young, there was a walkway right from the street into the courtyard of our building. You could come right into the yard through an alley. Opera singers would come down here every Sunday. They would sing their opera, and people would throw down quarters. A quarter was a lot of money back then. A slice of pizza used to cost a quarter, so if you had a dollar, you would have dinner.

My mom originally lived on the West Side at 144 Sullivan Street. She lived on the first floor with my grandmother, who didn't speak any English, and also my uncles. On the floor where I grew up lived my grandparents and my aunt and uncle with their kids, my cousins. Two flights up was another aunt and uncle and even more cousins. My godmother lived next door to my mom. Others lived here too that had extended family in the building. Everybody moved here.

All of my uncles were in World War II. In fact, when my uncle Dan came home from the war, he had PTSD and would sleep under the bed as if he was still in a foxhole. The building where they lived is across the street from St. Anthony's Church, which is the first Italian cathedral in America and where my parents had their wedding ceremony. It was tradition to get married in the parish the wife belonged to. My grandmother and my aunt Louisa sewed my mother's wedding gown and all the dresses for the wedding. We weren't devoutly religious, but we didn't eat meat on Fridays. I hated it, but I was an altar boy. I didn't like waking up early to do it, and I didn't even want to do the weddings, even though you got paid to do them. I did enjoy ringing the bells though.

A friend of mine who recently passed away, Frankie Bericci, owned Bericci's Bakery. His grandmother used to make all the bread. People in the neighborhood would bring their tables and chairs from their apartments down to the street and sit to have some bread and wine. Back in those days, you could leave your furniture or anything valuable down there and no one would touch it.

I vividly remember always washing the family dishes. I cleaned and dried them, and my mom and aunts taught me recipes along the way. I remember my grandmother had a big pan, and she would heat up oil and throw peppers into it. The whole building would smell like peppers. You always knew when she was cooking because you could smell it everywhere. My grandmother would be out in the hallway taking the peppers apart, and I would tease her and tell her not to cry. I knew she wasn't crying, it was just her eyes tearing up from the peppers, but I would run into the kitchen and put my face over the pot with the oil and peppers in it, and make myself tear up. I said, "Look, I'm crying too." She would come over and hug and kiss me.

I had a wonderful childhood like that. I even remember my first girl-friend. Her name was Diane. She lived across the street from me, and was the first girl I bought an ankle bracelet for. Our families knew each other. She was Italian/German. There were a bunch of blonde-haired girls living across the street, and I wound up with this girl. I guess you could call her my childhood sweetheart. What's funny is, later on, I found out I had been dating the aunt of Joe from Wisdom in Chains. He never even knew it. One Thanksgiving he is talking with his family at dinner about how he is going to go on tour. His aunt told him she used to date me, and he nearly shit his pants. He couldn't believe it. She even came to see my band one time with the family when we played in Jersey somewhere. Joe is so proud to tell people that his aunt dated me, whereas before, he only knew her as the aunt who made cookies for Thanksgiving.

I grew up playing all the New York street games like stoop ball, stickball, handball, and skelzy. We would make a little skelzy thing with a cork and fill the cork with wax or a penny to make it heavier. Skelzy was almost like marbles, but we made it our own little thing. It was back when neighborhoods were really these self-contained little communities with their own culture. We'd play our street games against other neighborhoods, so you'd get a little taste of their culture. You go up to Harlem, there are unique traditions up there. You go to Chinatown, there's Chinese culture. You want Jewish culture, you go over to Second Avenue. You come to Little Italy, there's a deep Italian culture. Whatever it is, you go to that community to experience their culture because you want the real deal. We all had that, especially back then. We were all friendly and good people. Oh, and the food…

Now, that's not to say that there weren't "elements" in our neighborhood. Guys that, you know, were made guys. You kept it separate. Business is business. Family is family. You might go to work and then get a phone call to do "something." My father would be like that. That is just the way it was at that time. He was never a made guy, he never got a "button," but he was involved. My father ran numbers a little bit, and as I mentioned, drove those guys around. I remember he had to disappear for a while when some guys got shot in the neighborhood. This was around 1972 when mob boss Joe Gallo was killed. Everyone from that time is dead now.

There were always a few younger guys who were sons of certain people, who would try to follow in their fathers' footsteps and use their clout for their own wants. But my father wasn't a big shot and I'm not either. My life definitely could've gone another way, and I could have wound up in the Mafia. I also could have wound up with two bullets in my head if I'd gone that way. Who would've been the one to kill me? Probably either a cousin or a best friend. That's just how things were. These were the people around me.

I remember my mom would sit in front of our building, and John Gotti would sometimes walk by. He and his friends always stopped to say hello to the old ladies out of respect on their way around the corner to the Ravenite Social Club. My mom spoke Italian and a little bit of English and was basically a housewife. She never wanted to teach me Italian though. I wanted to learn it, but as she told me, I was an American and needed to know English.

Overall, I was a good kid, but a terrible student. I liked having a good time, which for me, was getting together with my friends and hanging out in the basement. The boiler room kept us warm in the winter. We'd eat pizza, and once we got older, we would drink some beer and smoke a joint. My mom used to help me with homework, then my cousin Angela would help me. She used to get so frustrated with me that she would stab me in the arm with a pencil because I didn't listen. We still talk about it today when we get together.

I wasn't a troublemaker, but often got lumped in with the kids who were. One of my friends would throw something at our teacher and I wouldn't rat him out. The teacher would make all of us stay after school because of it. I left school after eighth grade. I went to high school for maybe one week, and then decided I couldn't do it. My mother told me I had to go to work if I wasn't going to school, so I went to work at a restaurant over by the Rockefeller Center skating rink. My cousin Terrance was the restaurant manager and got me the job as a busboy washing dishes. That was one of my first jobs besides a paper route or shining shoes.

I think what I have most inherited from my family is to be a good guy and be accepting of people. In order to get respect, you have to give respect. Of course, there are the traditions that come with growing up Italian: the Sunday family dinners, not ratting on people…those kinds of things. At the end of the day, I've always wanted to impress upon my son, and also Roger's little brother, Freddy, that no matter what, you have to follow your own path, use your own mind, and be a good example to others.

3

New Yorker

Sixty or so years down the road, this is still where I hang out. The Lower East Side is my 'hood. It's where me and my whole family come from. The LES wound up eventually blending into Little Italy, but back in the day, there really wasn't a difference between the Lower East Side, East Village, and Little Italy. It was all one big area until they paved Houston Street. Once Houston Street became a "real road," there was sort of a dividing line. The rows of houses were occupied by mostly Italian and Jewish people. As you went toward Second Avenue, it was the same. Eventually, people started moving from one end of Manhattan to the other, which changed the face of New York, because neighborhoods started becoming divided, with the exception of Chinatown. That area was always known as China-town, which it remains to this day. But the Lower East Side became separated into three separate neighborhoods.

Even though there became a division in the area, there was always a Jewish kid in my crew. There was always a Chinese kid in my crew; always a Puerto Rican kid in the crew. We used to bust each other's balls, teasing one another about our race or whatever. I'd call my friend Richie "Richie the Spic" 'cause he was Puerto Rican. He'd call me, "Skinny Vinnie the Guinea." You could never do that out loud today because everyone's such a pussy, but we knew we were friends and just had fun with it. No one was offended whatsoever. Now, if someone *outside* the crew said something like that to one of us, there would have been a serious problem.

I'll always reminisce about the neighborhood, the streets, opening up the fire hydrants in the summer, pulling fire alarms, and running away. Climbing up fire escapes from our clubhouse basements, hanging out with my friends on the roof… You know, "Tar Beach," overlooking the city. Of course, we had the pigeon coops and the water hose up there. I've even got a certain place on the ledge where I sit. I'm afraid of heights, but for some reason, I can sit there and not be scared. It's home.

Real New Yorkers are just different, and in case you haven't noticed, there are *a lot* of people here now who came from somewhere else, either to get a job or just be part of the excitement of this place. They want to

go out at night 'til all hours. They'd never have made it in the old New York. There's no grit to these people. They can't get with the algorithm, they don't get with the flow. They're walking like zombies, or looking at their phone every second, or just standing in the middle of the sidewalk. My god, move it along. Even the people in this building now; I've given up trying to be nice and making friends with them. They stay one or two years, then they're gone. You never see them again. They're not here to put down roots.

I had a friend come visit me from out of town, and all he wanted to do was go to Times Square to see the ball drop on New Year's Eve. I was like, "Really? There are all of these things we can go do in New York, and that's what you want to do?" He said it was his dream. So I reluctantly take him over there with a million fucking people, and we wind up in the middle of a riot. Some kids were snatching chains, and this police horse came barreling through this tight space, knocking all of us over and causing even more chaos. It was the worst. Tourists seem to love the meat-packing district too. It used to be absolutely dead. Nothing but transvestites and hookers over there. Now Paul McCartney's daughter has a thriving boutique right in the middle of it. There are hotels and expensive restaurants…. I'm still shocked.

We used to know everyone who owned a store or a business over here. Charlie used to have the candy store. He had sisters who had bouffant hairdos. They were twins and each had a poodle. I used to go in there to get my Halloween costumes. I'll never forget, they were three dollars. The big ones were five dollars. I always got the skeleton costume with the mask that made your face sweaty the minute you put it on. We knew the butcher, the baker, *and* the candlestick maker.

Shit, I even like doing jury duty here. I live close to the courthouses, so I can still wake up close to the time I need to be there and be perfectly on time. I grab the newspaper and a cup of coffee, and they pay you forty dollars to be there. Then I grab Chinese food and smoke a joint on the way home, and I'm good. It's a win-win. Usually, you're not there very long; maybe a day or two, and sometimes they send you home right when you sign in. Either way, I talk to everybody which is good and bad, because sometimes you run into the person willing to let someone go who just mugged a mother and her child. You know, they're siding with the robber. Once in a while, I have to set people straight.

It's like a broken record, but people (outside of New York) are still fascinated by our accents. They want you to say "coffee" to see how you pronounce it. *Kaw-fee*. Or "water." *Wah-ta*. It's annoying, but it's funny.

At the end of the day, I can go downstairs dressed the way I am now, in my pajamas, at 5:00 AM, in the middle of a snowstorm and get a container of milk or whatever I need. Maybe a couple hundred feet away. The city that never sleeps. I love that.

4

Music Fan

I'VE SEEN A LOT OF MUSIC and a lot of shows over the years. In the very early '70s, we would go to what was called Hilly's on the Bowery, which was a bum's bar. It later became world-famous as CBGB. Back then it started at fifteen cents for a shot and went all the way up to twenty-five cents a shot. You didn't need a lot of money back then to get drunk. I would also walk up to Max's Kansas City by myself. I would just go up to people everywhere and make friends; just start talking to them. I'd talk to anyone and everyone. When I had my Camaro, I would pull up to Max's and park it right on the sidewalk. The streets over there were dead, because the club was located in a Midtown business district which was basically closed at night. It was great.

Everybody was into glam in that Max's Kansas City scene. Not Mötley Crüe glam either, that old glitter and glam style. A lot of people used to wear wigs, and it wasn't just the New York Dolls. You'd see Andy Warhol and his whole crew of artists and models hanging out at Max's, but then,

later, you'd also have these more kinda punk bands like Pure Hell and the Dead Boys. Pure Hell was an all-Black band, and you had to see them, otherwise you might not have known about them. They didn't really get the same amount of attention back then that Bad Brains eventually got from the hardcore crowd.

I was lucky enough to see the beginning of punk rock in New York. I lived in the neighborhood where it was happening, so it was coming up all around me. New York truly had its own thing. I liked the Pistols and The Clash but, unfortunately, never got to see either of them in their heyday. People don't

really remember this, but there was actually kind of a divide between the bands that played Max's and the ones that played CBGB. I was always kind of disappointed that a lot of bands didn't play CBGB and only played at Max's, which had that snotty, pseudo-junkie, glam attitude. CBs seemed to be more about giving young bands a shot and less about image. On a whole other side, I did get to see Black Sabbath in the early '70s in an arena, even though I didn't really dig those giant arena shows. Aerosmith opened up for them and got booed off the stage, which I thought was kinda funny.

Back in the late '60s, very early '70s, there was a club called the Electric Circus on St. Marks Place. That's where I saw bands like Mandrill, Sly and the Family Stone, the Ohio Players, Joe Cocker, and Isaac Hayes. They had all the acts coming through there. Artists like Nina Simone would play there. I saw James Brown too. It was a mixed crowd of Blacks, hippies, drug dealers, and us neighborhood kids just cooling out. I ran around with a lot of the neighborhood guys—regular guys like me—and we would all go out to that club because, while we all loved rock, everybody liked soul music. I used to go there every Saturday night. That's when those acts would play. This was when I was still a rocker. The club was in a big, blue building, and there was no age limit. Since I lived nearby and knew everyone who worked the door, they welcomed me in. I can't believe how many incredible bands I saw there. It took me years before I really understood what I had seen, but that was downtown New York before punk rock. Not a lot of people got to see that. That's how I started becoming a true night-lifer.

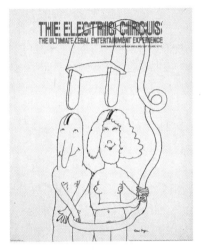 

5

Musician

(Part I)

AROUND FOURTEEN OR FIFTEEN, I bought my first guitar. It was a Fender Mustang that "fell off a truck," if you know what I'm saying. It was blue with a racing stripe on it and came with an alligator case, which would be worth a lot today to some collector.

My earliest "real" band was a neighborhood group called Black Angus. It was around 1973, before punk really ushered in a new era in New York. I was the only guitar player. My bandmates were Frankie and Sal, a.k.a. Sally. Sally lived around the corner from me, and was a big, fat guy. He was my bass player—my first real bass player—and he passed away. I still see his brother. The fire department had to take him out the window, because they couldn't get him down the stairs. I heard he'd passed, and they were taking him out the window, so I went over there. The fire department had closed the street down, and I saw my friend, Rob, who was his best friend. They were taking Sally out the window with a cherry picker, and it was a windy day. Sally was in the basket, and the basket was rocking back and forth. Rob says, "Vinnie, look—Sal, he's still rocking." We were laughing, we were crying, we were hugging. There's Sal rocking  away over there. He's been gone thirty years now. We were like the three goombahs. Which reminds me, I gotta call my friend Frankie. He's still alive. A hundred heart operations later, but he's still alive.

Anyway, we used to go up to the Bronx, around the Grand Concourse, to play. There were lots of gangs around back then: Savage Skulls, Dynamite Brothers, Ghetto Brothers…. I'm still friends with some of the Savage Skulls guys. Our band would play dance parties—mostly cover songs with a few originals thrown in. Fifties and sixties music with some rock stuff by The Who, Rolling Stones, and Led Zeppelin mixed in. The crowds up there loved us, because we were the band and we were neutral. We didn't wear colors like the gangs. There were also a couple of feasts that the band would play back then, including St. Loretta's and San Gennaro. We would even play for the neighborhood people if they had baptisms or birthday parties. Every neighborhood had a neighborhood band, so we were one of those.

After Black Angus, I bounced around the studios a lot, and, around 1974, I started playing in bands like Future Shock and The Slant. By 1977, I was in The Eliminators. We were a punk, sort of hardcore, band. To give you an example of what we sounded like, the Agnostic Front song "Power" was originally an Eliminators song. We started playing at Max's Kansas City. Believe it or not, there was one night we actually played there, CBGB, *and* A7: all three venues in one night. The Eliminators came about thanks to a combination of hanging around the studios and some ads in *The Village Voice*. I would hang around the rehearsal rooms and make friends with everybody. Those rehearsal rooms served a variety of purposes. You could use them to rehearse, of course, or if you wanted to have a party, you could rent a rehearsal room, hire a band to play, have some food delivered, and invite people to come.

I think when I first walked into Max's Kansas City, I knocked the fucking socks off of those people. I came in with my crew, and we weren't so glam looking. We had more of a chaos punk look, with studs and spiked bracelets. I had the hair and the dog chain around my neck. When we started playing there, people noticed we were different. Denise Mercedes from The Stimulators, which was a hugely important band in New York, dug it right away and told us she loved us. Denise was one of our earliest supporters.

We didn't play a lot of shows like that, though. Just some rehearsals and a couple of shows. I was doing everything by myself: driving us everywhere, making the flyers and the stickers. I even made stickers for the bands coming from out of town. Some people still have those stickers all these years later.

I remember, though, whenever I played, all these Chinese kids would come to see me play. They were members of the Ghost Shadows gang, who ruled Chinatown at the time. They were always in the news, but they were my friends. I used to hang in Chinatown a lot, and went to school with their family members.

The scene was really crazy. Punk was definitely crazy. There was the time I was standing outside a show when Mike Ness from Social Distortion threw a bottle towards me and some friends. It hit my leg and cut it open. That was during Social Distortion's Another State of Mind tour in 1982. Their very first tour. He had some beef or something; ran across the street and threw the bottle. He was just throwing it at the crowd, but it happened to hit me. Then, our bassist at the time, Diego and all those guys beat him up. I actually love Mike, and love seeing him to this day.

The Eliminators wound up being together for maybe three years, but you could see that, as time went on, the scene was changing from the glam thing to more aggressive punk. "Hardcore" punk. By 1979, 1980, a lot of that music was coming from the west coast: bands like Black Flag, X, and The Germs. The East Coast was coming up too, though, especially in the DC area, where you had bands like Minor Threat, SOA, Scream, and Bad Brains, who later moved up to NYC around 1981, '82. New York was a little slower to hardcore, probably because we didn't have the recording studios or the record labels the west coast had, but things changed, kids changed, and the scene changed. We had been straight-up

punks. We didn't have Dr. Martens yet or any of that; we had engineer or zipper boots. I think Harley Flanagan had the first pair of Dr. Martens in New York because he had gotten them over in Ireland when he toured there with The Stimulators.

But New York started to pick up steam as far as bands becoming harder and more aggressive. Groups started to come up like Kraut, The Mob, Reagan Youth, Nihilistics, Jesse Malin had Heart Attack.... I remember buying the Heart Attack *God is Dead* single from Jesse in front of CBGB when he was like fourteen years old for three dollars. I like the song, but I think the B-side, "Shotgun," is even better. I still tell him that.

Then there was Bad Brains, which was the band that made a lot of people want to start their own bands here in New York. They were great and their impact was big. A little later on came Agnostic Front and Murphy's Law, plus Cro-Mags even a little later. Those were the first three real bangers from New York.

I remember being there when Murphy's Law came up with their name in Uncle Al's apartment. It was Harley, Jimmy, Uncle Al, me, and a few other people. Uncle Al had a poster on his refrigerator that said something like, "ten things that can go wrong." All of a sudden, he says, "Why don't we just name ourselves 'Murphy's Law'?"

There were records coming out of New York now too; people were hearing hardcore, and promoters were booking it at places like CBGB and A7. And there was a community forming around it. I was already friends with all the staff and the bartenders at these places. During the day, because I lived around there, I'd pass by and ask what was going on for the night. I'd tell them that I was going for pizza or coffee and bring them back something. I had a good rapport with everyone at the clubs, and everybody knew I was from the neighborhood. Sometimes people would even yell out to me as they passed by in their cars. But as far as the bands, everyone was trying to speed up the twelve-bar blues and shrink it down. I said, "I can do that," and really started writing songs.

When I write, I try to think five, ten years down the road, and whether or not I think people will still like a song. That's what matters, right? If someone will connect with it and it lasts. To this day, I do like jamming to different kinds of music, including jazz. When the COVID pandemic hit, I had jazz apps on my phone and would play jazz all day long while I drank coffee. It's different and gave me some inspiration. I'd gotten so used to sitting down and playing guitar, that it felt weird when I put the strap back on. I had to get used to standing up and playing guitar again. Agnostic Front finally started booking tours, so I moshed around my kitchen for a bit with my guitar like a fourteen-year-old kid to get back in game shape.

6

Musician

(Part II—The Beginning of Agnostic Front)

AROUND THE SUMMER OF 1982, I did away with Zoo Crew and went full speed ahead with Agnostic Front. I came up with the name because I wanted a statement. I wanted something real, something you could believe in. When I look at a band onstage, I ask myself a few questions: "Do I believe in this band?" "Are they there for the scene, are they down for the cause?" Some bands are around for the short-term, maybe a few months and then they break up. How can you believe in them? People say it's a lifestyle, but it's also a belief for me. If you don't believe in your own band or the music you are playing, I don't have any use for you.

So, "Agnostic Front" has two parts to the name: the first part is the belief part; trying to figure out what you believe. A front is your stance or your point of view. You could be in doubt, question authority, and then take a position. It could be political, social, or religious. I know when you look at it in the dictionary, it's listed under religion, but it is an ambiguous name. I looked at it from a lot of different directions.

The first version of Agnostic Front got started on the dance floor, really. That's pretty much where I met everyone. I'd see how they did their thing out there, and if I liked what they were doing, I'd approach them. Once I wanted to start the band, I got Raybeez to join first, then

I met Diego and John Watson. No one except me had any gear, and no one was a musician. They couldn't even follow the notes, a.k.a. "dots," on the guitar neck. That is what I still call them today. Mike Gallo will say to me, "What do you mean you follow the dots?" I point to them and tell him, "Well, that's an A-major, and that's the B-flat."

The first Agnostic Front show we played, which was billed as "Zoo Crew," was with those guys: Watson, Diego, and Raybeez. There's a flyer floating around somewhere that Watson made for it. At the time, I was the only one with a driver's license, phone number, and some equipment. We had to make a bass drum head out of a cardboard pizza box, and used a garbage can cover for a cymbal. I loved it because it felt so  street, so real. You can't get more real than pizza boxes and garbage cans.

That show didn't have much of an audience. Everyone was using my equipment, and I was the only one who had a bass. I had to give Diego my bass, along with all the distortion boxes and cables. I will never forget when Watson would throw down the mic and get on the dance floor. Then Diego would throw my Gibson bass on the floor. It looked like an SG, and is probably rare today. I'd stay onstage with Raybeez trying to keep the beat, which was a hard thing to do with Ray. He played like he was a wind-up toy. Diego was such a hothead. He would throw the bass down and fight with people in the pit. He would mosh really hard. One time at a show in DC, we wound up in a stupid fight. Well, Diego and Watson did. I was in it for maybe a minute before them. I was not for that kind of stuff. I'm here to play, make friends, and sell T-shirts.

All that said, I had written a bunch of songs, but couldn't really get it together with that group of guys. They weren't serious. They didn't look at music the way I did, because they weren't musicians. I didn't care at first, because these were the people I wanted to be in the band with, and who I thought would help get us some attention, but we couldn't make it happen at all. But I was still gung-ho about having this band. It meant a lot to me. There's even a flyer out there somewhere that says, "If you don't come to our show, Vinnie says you'll be marked."

Watson was the first person to leave the band, so we had Jimmy the Russian, who was in a band called Virus, come in to sing. Then I got Adam Mucci to play bass. Now, I had already seen Roger play bass in The Psychos, and I really wanted him to be in the band. He danced all crazy at the shows, too, which made me want him more. I had Adam go over and tell him I wanted him to join, so Roger came over to talk to me. He was a little confused because he was the bass player in The Psychos, and Adam was already our bass player. But I loved watching Rog on the dance floor. We chatted, and at the end of the talk, Roger said he would do it; he would be our singer. Thank God, because otherwise, I wouldn't still be talking about this band this many years later.

So now, we are in 1982, and Agnostic Front is me, Roger, Adam, and Ray. It was a lot of fun. We rehearsed in this basement boiler room over on Grand Street, and we started playing a bunch with bands like Urban Waste, The Psychos, Ultra Violence, Virus, and others.

When we first started touring, we went as far south as DC, as far north as Boston, and as far west as Ohio. We all packed in a van together. When we went to Ohio that first time, I think we played with The Dark and Negative Approach. Wendy from Guillotine took a picture of us with pirate hats on when we stopped at a Long John Silvers, because they were giving away pirate stuff.

At those out-of-state shows, people would bring their friends. We were the out-of-state band/guests, and you gotta make friends with the people that are around. Ask them questions, see if they need anything. I was always helpful like that. I remember at one show, a guy in another band needed an amp, so I told him he could use my amp. People acted surprised that I lent the guy my amp. I looked at it like, this guy has to get up there and play the show. I'm gonna get up there after him, so what's the difference? We're playing the same show, and I want it to be good for everybody.

Early on we adopted a skinhead look, but it was a New York hardcore version of it, kinda like the way the Fordham Baldies were, that kind of attitude. It wasn't the traditional English skinhead kind of thing. It wasn't about Fred Perry, because, you know, we didn't play tennis. It was a different take. It was just: Everyone shave your head; whoever you are, whatever you are. Come join our gang. But when I say "our gang," I don't mean it to be a gang of violence. Our skinhead people from the Lower

East Side, we had our share of fights and everything, but it wasn't a thing where we were going out and fighting people for no reason. It was a fun thing, that's all. It was our little culture. We all shaved our heads and were really the first skinhead band, at least in New York. Even our roadies had shaved heads. We wound up introducing it to a lot of people around the country once we toured. We did get shit for how we looked, though, and what people assumed skinhead meant to us, but we had a Cuban, a Russian, and an Italian guy in the band. Sure, there was some influence from the English skinheads, but we didn't completely adopt their style. It was New York style. We did our own thing. Like, out west, punks were into dyed hair and mohawks. Here, we had no hair. They did the circle pit, we did the mosh. But there was no such thing as prejudice to us. We wore boots, had our chain wallets, and rolled up our jeans. When we got out of the New York area and saw what people's perception of us was, I was surprised. Some people thought we were basically Skrewdriver (an English neo-Nazi band) but from New York. I don't ever want people assuming anything or judging me, but that happened a lot. I don't judge people. I come in peace and am here for a good time. I just wanted to entertain people, drink beer, and pick up girls. We weren't pushing any political ideology whatsoever. For me and the band, our music was more about social stuff and unity within our scene: Black, white, punk, skin. It was always meant to be inclusive. I wasn't interested in offending anyone. The idea was for us to come together for a common cause.

Everything about Agnostic Front—the music, the image, the way we dressed, the way we represented—was hardcore punk. There was an edge to us. We walked it like we talked it. Unity was so important to us. We tried to start a BYO (Better Youth Organization) chapter in New York. However, early on, a lot of people didn't believe in the cause. I treated guys on the scene like I treated my band: "Do you believe in this? Do you believe in the movement? Are you my brother, my sister, my friend?" In order to have a friend, you have to be a friend. Help someone if you can; go out of your way.

I would help people. I actually gave Sindi from the Lunachicks guitar lessons. I'm no guitar teacher, but I know the basics and could play. I would get people started, and if they weren't good, it wasn't a big deal. That's not what it was about. It was a great period in time. I was at every show. I enjoyed making friends and making events happen. I'd book a show, have my friends play, and dance to every band. Sometimes, because it seemed like the "punk" thing to do, people would sit down on the stage and watch the band. That's disrespectful. I hate seeing people sitting down while I'm on stage. Stand up and watch the band! When I would be playing and someone was sitting down on the stage, I would kick them right in the kidney and yell, "Get off my fucking stage! Don't sit on my fucking stage!" You shouldn't do that to anybody. You rehearse, work hard just to have somebody sit there?! Get the fuck out of here. The least you could do is just stand up. Don't sit there like you're bored. Nowadays, you get some kid texting in a corner. It's the new version of

sitting down. Who checks their fucking texts when a band is on?! Get in the pit if you want to support and enjoy the band, don't text.

A lot of people doubted my band and myself, especially as a guitar player. They were usually musician types, but they didn't understand that it wasn't what we were about. It wasn't about being the greatest guitar player, it was about the message. It's about the band. It's about what you believe. I know a lot of great, skilled guitar players who aren't doing anything today.

7

Recording Artist

(Part I, 1983–1984)

THE IDEA TO RECORD THE *United Blood* single came about from the songs the guys and I had been rehearsing. We were playing them at shows, and at that time, a lot of NY bands started coming out with EPs, so we decided we needed to record the songs. We recorded it at Don Fury's in my neighborhood, three blocks from my house.

We did everything by hand back in the day. I had been making Agnostic Front stickers, which was smart, because there were a lot of bands coming up, and it helped people remember us. We had the records pressed and bought the sheets of covers that we would cut, fold, and paste together, all by hand. Luckily, I had a lot of people that would come to my apartment to help us. This was still when my whole family lived in the building, so they would hear us and bring us food. We sold some to a few record stores and at the shows. We sold them to whoever would help us. Even sold about fifty of them to Jack Flanagan from The Mob, who sold them for us. Everyone was helping.

The reaction to *United Blood* was really good. We came with that New York sound, as did bands like Urban Waste, The Abused, The Mob, and Cause for Alarm. What made it so identifiable as the New York sound was the slower dance parts, the mosh parts. The west coast had the fast,

circle-pit style. New York did it differently. It's funny: when I watch a
band like Madball doing the old
Agnostic Front songs now, I feel
like they've modernized it and per-
fected it even more. Sometimes I
can't believe I actually wrote those
songs. Recently, I got up and sang
"United Blood" at an H2O show,
and seeing the crowd react the way
they did this many years later was
amazing. These kids weren't even

born back then, and yet they're singing along with me. That's a great
achievement as far as I'm concerned. They know the song, believe in the
song, and the main thing is, the song is still relevant to them.

By 1983, hardcore had become a "thing" all over the place, and a lot
more people were starting to show up at shows, especially at CBGB.
Plus, there were just a lot more shows. The New York scene was growing, plus Boston, DC, Connecticut, New Jersey.... Agnostic Front was
starting to get a following thanks to the
EP—and us playing those songs live.
People could take the band home with
them now. However, I knew we couldn't
go on with the lineup we had on *United
Blood*. Not too long after, we decided to
do a full album. We recorded *Victim in
Pain*, which ultimately became the blue-
print for New York hardcore.

Enter Rob Kabula. He was from Jersey and played bass in Cause
for Alarm. He and I were friends, and he was also friends with Roger.
Kabula wound up in the band, as did Dave Jones, who was the drummer
from Mental Abuse.

I hooked up with Dave Parsons at the Rat Cage to release *Victim in Pain*. Everyone knew Dave, who was very eccentric. I knew him just from hanging around. I originally met Dave back at Max's Kansas City, and then he bought a record store and I bought records from him. Dave started the record label and we just went along with him. He put out a lot of great stuff, including that early Beastie Boys record. Years later, I was at my tattoo shop and I see someone looking through the window. He opens the door and goes, "Do you know who I am?" I realized it was Dave, who by now had transitioned to female and went by the name "Daisy." I said, "Dave, get the fuck in here!" Everyone in the shop was like, "Who the fuck is that?" and I told them, "That's the guy who put out my first album!" I think he died during a sex change operation.

At first, we didn't have the money to track and mix the album, so we played a show at CBs in order to raise money, and put Don Fury's band, Balls, on the bill so he'd record it. I rented out a sixteen-track machine, and we got whatever the discount was because we had put his band on that show. It only took a few days to record *Victim in Pain*. I mean, the album is only around fifteen minutes long, but for us, it didn't matter. It was our album. It's the sound of New York.

I pass the building where Don Fury's studio used to be all the time. It's a Buddhist Temple now, but Don Fury made a career off that record. Everyone went to his place after *Victim in Pain*. I laugh because everything on the record is so off, but other bands wanted to have that sound. It was like, "Can we have that piece of stale bread too?"

To this day, I hear people say, "When I first heard *Victim in Pain*, wow!" It's funny, because the timing is off, the tempo is off, the tuning is off.... Let's just say, the recording is a little shaky. It's literally our fifteen minutes of fame. I felt like, if you're going to play guitar or play hardcore, it's got to have a certain sound, it's got to be a certain speed. Yeah, you can have your fast and slow stuff, but there's got to be a hook in there. It's got to be raw, but there has to be something to hold on to. And it doesn't

have to be perfect, it has to be from the heart. I think it's the greatest mistake I ever made.

When I got the finished record and it was a gatefold, I knew immediately that this was a hardcore album, the way a hardcore record should be. Roger came up with the cover concept. It was such an interesting time because, although the message in our lyrics was pretty clear, thanks to the skinhead thing a lot of people somehow didn't understand what we meant. They got stuck on the word "Front," because of England's National Front and its association with (neo-Nazi) British skins. For us, it was simple, and was meant to represent our point of view and where we were coming from. I never wanted just a band name with Agnostic Front. I wanted a statement, but I never wanted to be painted into a corner. I wanted to be the paint. Also, the cover with the SS soldier made a lot of people question what we were actually about. But in the end, when people opened up that gatefold and saw the band and the way we were dressed, everyone was like, "I *have* to see that band." Everything about it was great: the name, the cover, the music, the live photo inside.... That's what every band should strive for, and let's just say, Agnostic Front was on the map now.

8

Recording Artist

(Part II, 1986)

WITHOUT EVEN REALIZING IT, or paying much attention to it, Agnostic Front had become part of the crossover hardcore/metal scene without really trying to. *Victim in Pain* had a lot of fast songs on there, and that seemed to be what the kids wanted at that time. Metal bands were playing fast by then too: Metallica, Slayer, Anthrax…. They heard us, DRI, Corrosion of Conformity, and all the other bands who were playing fast and added it to their sound. They started coming to the matinees too. We had become friends with Scott Ian from Anthrax, and even the

Metallica guys came down to see Broken Bones in the afternoon before they played a show at L'Amour. I wasn't there but I remember hearing about Kirk Hammett from Metallica coming to CBs to play with the Crumbsuckers, and Tommy Carroll from Straight Ahead spit on him, calling him a "rock star" and telling him to get off the stage. The crossover didn't always go smoothly.

Even though we hadn't recorded it yet, the next AF album had the working title: A Growing Concern. I'll admit, I was a little in denial at the time, because this was the era where the "real" musician came into what we had been doing (with hardcore), and, in a way, ruined the old hardcore music. Live-performance-wise too. Technicality limits what you can present on stage. In the punk rock movement, people were cutting themselves on stage, bleeding, throwing themselves on the floor, rolling around in glass…throwing up. People were becoming afraid to express themselves because they were scared they might look foolish. They were afraid to get out of that shell. You just have to crack that egg! But these metal guys knew how to play guitar. They were faster and louder. It was rough for me at first because I'm not that kind of guitar player. I'm a punk rocker.

Sometimes, you just have to take that leap, and make the jump; just like from punk to hardcore, now it was hardcore to crossover. I had seen a crossover happen before with glam turning into punk. You have to keep up with what's happening. Hardcore moved to what I call "slip and fall," because these guys were very slippery on the guitar. It was very smooth, and it was another style I had to learn to play instead of the chug or the gallop. I had to get my right hand on the guitar to stay tighter. I'll never forget, when I was doing it in the beginning, they actually duct taped my hand to the guitar.

Back in the day, the equipment was also different. People used cheap guitars and borrowed other people's amps. Now, everyone has all the newest stuff. Hardcore bands use the same gear as Metallica. And nobody used an electric tuner back then. You used a little tuning fork and tuned by ear. I suppose it's just a different time. It's fine to follow tradition, but if you want to be a pioneer, you have to make your own path; you have to update the sound.

When it came time to do *Cause for Alarm*, there was some leftover music from *Victim in Pain*, but we were looking for new ideas. I wrote a lot of halves of songs, including "The Eliminator," and some arrangements. At this time, the lineup was different again. Kabula left. Dave had left a while earlier. We toured with Jimmy Colletti in the band from sometime in 1984 for probably two years. By now, we had the same manager as Carnivore, Crumbsuckers, and Whiplash—Connie Barrett. We'd heard that Louie Beato and Peter Steele were fans of Agnostic Front. I became friends with Louie, and wound up doing backup vocals on the Carnivore albums. He eventually agreed to play drums on our album because we didn't have a drummer at the time. That's how Pete became involved with Agnostic Front, through my relationship with Louie. We used to go out to Brooklyn to rehearse, and Pete helped us out with some lyrics.

Obviously, there was a whole thing about the lyrics he wrote for the song "Public Assistance." For the record, it was never about race, it was

about a segment of poor people taking advantage of the system. But of course, the big, bad skinhead band has to be racist. Thanks, Phil Donahue! There always has to be a bad guy. There has to be someone to point to and say, "They're doing it wrong." I still have to defend myself from that sometimes. It's like when they bring up peoples' tweets from years ago, like there's no chance that they'll grow or learn or change. It's too much sometimes.

I remember one night, Peter played Roseland with Hatebreed. They were going to have an afterparty somewhere in the city, and Mini KISS was supposed to play (an all-dwarf KISS cover band in full costumes and makeup). I was on Hatebreed's bus, and we were trying to set it up so that Mini KISS would try to mug Peter because he was so tall. It would have been fuckin' funny!

So, me, Jamey Jasta, Peter, and some manager guy get in a cab and we're going to the afterparty. Jamey is getting ready to pay the cab driver, and Peter is in the front seat of the cab because he's taller than all of us. Jamey, the manager guy, and I get out, and Peter is still sitting in the cab.

We're trying to get Peter to get out of the cab, and I'm trying to get him mugged by Mini KISS. I was telling them to be ready to mug him the minute he walks in. Peter doesn't know any of that, and he's just sitting in the cab, not wanting to go in. The driver is telling him he has to get out, and that there are cars behind him beeping and trying to get past. We can't get him out of the car. He is stubborn and won't go in.

Now there's a line of cars behind us, and people are starting to gather around. Jamey tells the cab driver to just take us back to Roseland. So the cab goes back to Roseland, and we get Peter out of the cab somehow. We take him to Jamey's bus, and

Peter is just sitting and talking about the old days. Peter eventually goes back to his bus, which is just ahead of Jamey's, and then everybody goes back down to the Mini KISS afterparty. Afterward, I jump in a cab and head home.

That was the last time I saw Peter. A few years later he passed away. He was a good guy and friend.

Cause for Alarm came out, and a lot of people were surprised by what it sounded like. We gained a lot of new fans—lots of different people coming to see us, but there was also a lot of backlash from some of our hardcore fans. They thought we had gone too far with the metal influence. But we finally had the record company behind us, and people were paying attention to the band. We started to play bigger shows with bands like Slayer. We finally played L'Amour opening for Exodus, which, up until then, didn't feel like the right place for us to play. We were becoming a much more popular band. I'm glad we did it, though, and made the jump.

9

Recording Artist

(Part III, 1987–Present)

FOR ONE REASON OR ANOTHER, people wouldn't stay in the band for very long. It may have been due to the constant transition of the music, but also we weren't internationally known. We were a somewhat nationally known band that traveled around in a van. You know, that's not for everyone.

Naturally, by 1987, the lineup changed again. Steve Martin of the Boston band Straw Dogs joined us on guitar. Steve is actually from Long Island, but at the time was going to school in Boston. Also added was Will Shepler on drums and Alan Peters on bass, both of whom came from Pittsburgh. Agnostic Front was a whole new group, and we were going to go into the studio to record *Liberty and Justice For....*

We weren't going to do something similar to *Cause for Alarm* again. We all brought different styles to the band and different songwriting ideas. The song that I think saved that album was our version of "Crucified." It's an Iron Cross song and was like an anthem to a lot of people. Most people hadn't heard it before we did it, and we'd been playing it live for years. There were only about three hundred copies of the Iron Cross record out there, but now, anyone can hear their version since it is on YouTube. Even my mother always thought that was an Agnostic Front song. She would say, "Look at the skinhead band, that's my son!"

I will say that musically, with this record, I made another jump reluctantly. I still wanted the music to be similar to *Victim in Pain*, but, by then, it wasn't just the band involved in making the record anymore. We had producers, and the record company seemed to care a little bit after the success of *Cause for Alarm*. The contract said the album needed to be at least forty-five minutes in length, but as long as we were over thirty minutes, we thought that was okay. No matter the length, a song needs to have its own character. It should have its own little thing. There's a fine line between that and it getting boring, so we tried to make sure it wasn't boring.

Something I accept is that change is necessary in music. I go along with it even if it's not 100 percent my cup of tea. I always want to go back to the *Victim in Pain* sound when I was the only guitar player, or even when I had another guitar player that played like me, you know, the old-fashioned way.

Cause for Alarm caught the record company a little off guard because at the time, the crossover scene was what was in style, and we fit right into it. Then *Liberty and Justice For...* came out, and the next big wave of straight edge was happening. Bands like Youth of Today were having their time in the spotlight. They did a good job and I'm a fan. Agnostic

Front bridged that gap a little bit, but that was the sound I liked, and now that it was coming back around, it seemed that I had been right all along. People seemed to like the album, though, and we were keeping the band moving. But, by the time we were done touring on the album, there was a little bit of a lull. We weren't really sure where to go next, or even who would be in the band.

Around 1989, Howie Abrams and Steve Martin, who was still in the band, decided to start a label out in Queens called In-Effect Records. They actually started it to do a better job with bands like ours, which were kinda caught between all the death and thrash metal bands on Combat Records. They were pretty popular, but still very underground. I mean, I love a band like Obituary, but we just weren't the same. We had been playing the same clubs as those bands, and drawing more people, but Combat definitely didn't put the same amount of effort into our band. But now, Agnostic Front was the premiere band at In-Effect Records. The label cared a lot about the band, and unlike Combat, they gave us the attention we deserved. We didn't mind working hard, we were used to it.

The band moved from Combat to In-Effect and talk began of recording a live album at CBGB. The owner, Hilly Kristal, gave me the blessing to go ahead and do it. I knew Hilly for a long time, even before Agnostic Front. I used to show up at load-in for the Sunday matinee shows and bring him coffee and cookies. Roger was a barback there too.

We decided to move ahead with the live album. It was gonna be sort of a greatest hits album of our earlier albums. Agnostic Front was *the* band at CBGB by this time. I think The Ramones actually only played there maybe three times. That club was ours now. I don't know of any band that played there more than us. Plus, we did more benefits for CBGB than any band. It was definitely something else to record there. It was a great day. I was very grateful seeing how many people came out for the recording. Thankfully, the *Live at CBGB* album put a lot of attention back on AF.

Now the '90s were coming in, and the old hardcore sound was kind of dying again. There were so many different styles of music mixing in with hardcore now. We were ready for another change. Craig Setari was in Youth of Today at the time, but I remember him from his first band, NYC Mayhem, with Tommy Carroll and Gordon Ancis. Gordon's uncle was Rodney Dangerfield, and he was in the band for a while too. Gordon, not Rodney! I used to see Craig all the time and watch him jump around while he played. I love that in a hardcore show, when everyone is jumping around with the tempo of the music, in sync with what the band is doing. Craig and Ray Cappo were fun to watch. Plus me, Cappo, and Porcell have the big, Italian noses, so I felt like we had something in common. At one point, I told Craig that he was great and was going to be in my band one day. I loved him from the minute I met him.

Eventually Alan Peters left the band, and I needed a bass player. That's where Craig comes in. Roger went away during this time to serve his sentence. We did that matinee benefit for Roger the first week of January in 1989 at CBGB. In just a couple of days, he was going away to serve his time. The show was called No Justice, Just Us. We shot the live video at the same time for "Anthem," which George Seminara directed. Roger had a buzz cut for that show. He'd cut his hair because he was going to jail. Luckily, he had a lawyer that helped him and only served around two years instead of all the time he was sentenced to. But now, Agnostic Front was on hold...and so was I.

Once Roger was released, the band started back up, and we went on tour. Steve wound up leaving, and Matt Henderson, who was from Minneapolis, wound up joining AF. This was around 1991. Matt had been in Blind Approach, who we had played with at some point. He was always a good kid and a good guitar player. He went to Berklee College of Music in Boston for guitar.

We did a few shows, and there were some songs we played instrumentally before they wound up with lyrics. I think at the time, they were called "Back Burner," "Hard B," and "Leftover." With Matty, I had

to learn how to play the guitar differently again with a new picking style. It was a new era of Agnostic Front with *One Voice*. Rap music was hot on the music scene; the crossover thing was kind of going out, and there was a new thing people called "metalcore": metal bands with a hardcore attitude. The look and choreography was hardcore, but the sound was metal. We had to adapt again.

One of the things we did with the *One Voice* lineup was film the home video at the fourth Hardcore Superbowl. It was Agnostic Front, Sick of It All, and Gorilla Biscuits, also directed by George Seminara. It was the first time people had really seen Matty in the band. That show was a reestablishing of the old—plus many of the new—hardcore bands from New York all together. You had a great straight-edge band, then a hot up-and-comer like Sick of It All with us at the top. People love that video. There were probably twenty-five hundred, three thousand people there and it really showed the different styles of hardcore in New York at the time. Kids all over the world bring it up to me and want to talk about it.

10

Scapegoat

AROUND THE MID-'80S, *Maximum RockNRoll* magazine out in San Francisco and its founder Tim Yohannan targeted the New York scene—especially Agnostic Front, as if we were all that was wrong with hardcore punk. Tim labeled many in the New York hardcore community as Nazis and thugs. Being that the 'zine was considered the hardcore punk bible of the time, these accusations seriously messed with the reputations of many of the New York bands as they toured across America and around the world.

Man, that *Maximum RockNRoll* did a real number on us—and a lot of other New York bands. Some people are just too much, and that guy, Tim Yohannan, was too much. It became a real pain in the ass. I tried to have a conversation with him, and there was no talking to him. There was no room for anyone to have an opinion different from his.

Maximum RockNRoll would publish these scene reports, and the New York report wasn't about the bands anymore, it was about the "fascist skinhead problem," which New York never had. It was gaslighting.

Tim was three thousand miles away listening to people who, in some cases, he'd never even met. He was comparing us to people in Europe. That's like comparing Will Smith to a gangster rapper. Basically, we were crazy kids who shaved our heads and ran around like nuts. I mean, Jimmy Gestapo: really? A Nazi?! The best headline I've ever read was "Jimmy Gestapo Beats Up Nazis" after he had a confrontation with neo-Nazi skinheads in Florida. He's not a Nazi, stupid! It's an old, crazy punk-rock name like "Johnny Rotten." Was Johnny actually rotten? No. Jimmy's a great guy. A little nuts, but a great guy.

There's always got to be a bad guy, but you have to find a common denominator. And there are always gonna be people who won't let that happen, because it doesn't sell the way bullshit does. Like I said, I tried talking to that guy at *Maximum RockNRoll* years ago. I tried to be rational and polite, but he wasn't interested. I will always accept your ideas even if I don't agree with you. I try to understand where you're coming from, but you shouldn't let these things come between you. I mean, would you hate me if I was Black? Would you hate me if I was Chinese? Would you hate me if I was gay? Would you hate me if I was transgender? Why would you hate me for being a free-thinking person with whatever political beliefs or religious beliefs or anything I may have? Why would you hate me for any of those reasons?

11

Elder

(Madball)

In 1989, Madball released a seven-inch record. It was me, Roger, Willie, and Freddy, who was only twelve years old at the time. The name Madball came from people pissing Freddy off. When he got mad, he would make this crazy face, and I would say, "Look at him. He looks like a Madball, leave him alone." I couldn't see picking on the kid. I don't like hazing or any of that stuff, but it was funny and the name stuck.

We went to Don Fury's and recorded some stuff, just like Agnostic Front had. Then Roger took the recording to In-Effect Records out in Queens. He told Howie that he wanted to play him something. It had about seven minutes of music on it, and Howie loved it. He said it reminded him of *United Blood*. The cassette Roger played Howie turned into the *Ball of Destruction* seven-inch. He decided to put it out a few months after the big benefit for Roger's legal expenses, and it became more popular than we expected. While Agnostic Front was jumping around with our sound, Madball reminded everyone of that old style: that Negative Approach, *United Blood*-era AF sound.

We started playing some shows with Madball. Freddy's voice was that of an angry child; the guitar roared and the drums had a tribal pounding sound. It had all the New York flavor thrown in there with a raging adolescent voice, and people loved it. That's where the AF family tree really started to grow. People became very aware of Madball outside the US too.

Another Madball single came out around '92 called *Droppin' Many Suckers*. Roger had left the band, and we had a new bassist, Hoya, who Freddy knew from Queens. He was the perfect guy to add to the band.

Fast-forward to 1994. Madball is now Freddy, Hoya, me, and Matty. Howie Abrams from In-Effect Records was now at Roadrunner Records. The band went up to the Roadrunner office and said we wanted to tour and make records. Howie told us that if we were serious about becoming a "real band," he was in. The band went up to Rhode Island and did *Set It Off*. It was modern hardcore. The album took off in Europe and was a big deal. We played the Dynamo Festival in Holland in the

summer of 1995. It was huge! By the time the headliners played, there were 120,000 people there from all over the world. There were already about 75,000 people there to watch us play at noon. They really knew the Madball songs and were singing along with Freddy. One kid grabbed

the mic when Freddy went out into the crowd and wouldn't let go of it. Freddy actually challenged the guy to meet him after the show. I don't think they ever met up.

Around the time Madball released *Set It Off*, Biohazard had become huge, especially overseas. They were in all the magazines, and were all over MTV Europe. This was the first exposure to something hardcore for a lot of people over there.

Madball was playing festivals and shows together with Biohazard, and in Europe, everybody from New York was from Brooklyn. We never came off like that. We were from New York. We're underground. Before there was Brooklyn, there was New York. New York is number one, and always will be number one. That's the end of that.

12

Touring Musician

(Part I)

FOR A WHILE, I was a longshoreman on the docks over on the west side. I didn't like it, but somebody got me the job, if you know what I mean. It was kind of a no-show job. I never wanted to go to that place, but I had to go—show up, at least—because my mother would've killed me if I didn't. Also, I didn't want to embarrass the guy who got me the job.

Early on, I used to show up looking like a fucking punk: blood and makeup on me, fucking half in the bag. I was crazy then. I used to park my '69 Camaro in the loading bay, and I couldn't have cared less about the job, but let's just say I was protected. All these straight-laced guys with wives and kids who worked at the site, they couldn't get with me. I was like, "Excuse me, you do your job and let me do my job. Am I bothering you?" I eventually became the boss of some of the workers and was cool with everyone. I let them do pretty much whatever they wanted. I would let this one guy drink: "Sure, go in the back and have a drink." One guy used to live kinda far away, so I'd say, "Don't worry about it. As long as you come in here on time, I'll punch you out and you can leave early." Another guy would gamble. I'd tell him, "Put five bucks in for me." I actually knew the bookie that would come by. "Any number you want, I'll split it with you." I was cool like that. But these guys were jealous of me, and jealousy is a self-inflicted wound. You've got nobody to blame but yourself when you're jealous.

At one point in 1984, Agnostic Front was supposed to go on tour, and I finally said, "I'm gonna fix these jealous motherfuckers." I had a baseball bat, and Roger was waiting outside with the van. It was a Friday. I got my pay, and I cracked about four or five guys' heads open with the bat. Then I just got in the van and we left. That was that. That was my last day. I called my mom to let her know I was heading to Atlanta and left in the van with Roger.

We'd all cram into that van and usually had a dog with us too. Thank god for Roger—great carpenter. He built the inside of the van so that we had the equipment underneath, and we all slept on top of one mattress. I used to hug (longtime AF friend and roadie) Frenchie like a body pillow. We would spoon. It's why I still eat ravioli with a spoon to this day.

In Atlanta, I ran into a preacher in a little Baptist church. The church was across the street from a club called The Matrix, which has since burned down. I said hello to the preacher and took my shoes off, my hat, whatever I had to do. I was always respectful to everyone. He asked how I was, and right away, he knew I was from New York. I told him I was a Catholic. He asked if I wanted to come into the church. I told him I did and stood in the back, just being respectful. After a little while, I left the church to call my mother from a pay phone just outside. "Hey, Ma. How you doing?" She goes, "What did you do?! I had to call so-and-so to straighten everything out because of what you did!" After my mother gave me the ear-beating, I was shaking like a leaf. I kind of peeked back into the church, and the priest waved to me, so I went back in and sat in the corner. I stayed around five minutes and prayed for myself: "Please, don't let my mother kill me!"

When Agnostic Front first toured, every other show would get canceled. We'd stay in friends' apartments or on whoever's floor we could for multiple days. Bands would put us up, and we'd play little places like VFW halls, garages…anything we could get. We made our own merchandise and show flyers. Everything by hand. It was nothing like it is today, and I don't regret any of it. I lived on three dollars a day. I could get a couple hot dogs and a Big Gulp for ninety-nine cents. That was breakfast, lunch, and dinner. I'm still that way. I'll sleep on the floor somewhere if I need to. I don't care what I have to do because I enjoy playing so much. I truly *have* to play. A big thing I think helped me was that I was a little older and had been a punk rocker before. While I always appreciated anyone who would book us, or let us stay at their house, we would never know what to expect, especially the first time in some of these American towns.

Agnostic Front was one of the first New York hardcore bands to tour cross country. I believe only Cause for Alarm had done it before us… maybe Reagan Youth too. People would often think a certain way about us because of our shaved heads and boots. But then they'd meet us and would realize we weren't any of the stuff they thought we were.

One time we were playing in Louisiana at a club called The Soiled Dove. It turned out to be a lesbian bar, but going in, we had no idea. We were loading in and these women were playing pool in the club and giving us dirty looks. Some lady went up to them and told them, "Leave

them boys alone." I was like, "Wow!" I had to collect money from the lady at the end of that night in their little office. We thought we were these macho guys from New York, but I was terrified that I was going to get beat up. The show went well, though; there were maybe thirty people there. It was definitely a whole different thing from what we were used to.

When it comes to touring, I always tell people in bands, make friends with anyone and everyone while on the road. Could be the crew, club staff, bartenders, security, promoters.... Sometimes there are issues, whether it is money, or booking, or someone at the club is an asshole. Things happen. But you have to keep a cool head and be on the right side of history. It's the same thing with me onstage. I run around waving at people, blowing kisses, helping people up, or helping people off the stage. If somebody falls and gets hurt, I will stop playing to help them because I get scared and don't want to see anyone injured. Personally, I just love going to new places, eating the food and making friends.

One of the craziest shows we played early on had over four thousand people in attendance. It was at the Olympic Auditorium in Los Angeles with The Exploited and U.K. Subs. What a show that was. Rioting, helicopters, fires burning, cars overturned.... Roger and I had gone into the bathroom before the show, and a bunch of guys came in wanting

to fuck with us because we were skinheads. So who comes in? Louiche from Suicidal Tendencies. He told the guys that we were his friends, so we became cool with the Suicidals.

Like I said, I just like having a good time. I drink with everybody. I'll eat any kind of food. It doesn't matter to me. I want to know about *you* too, you know what I mean? Of course, everybody wants to know about me, or New York. I'm the guy in the band,

and people look up to musicians. I have to blaze the trail for others to follow and conduct myself in a way others might want to emulate.

When we're playing, people can come up on stage and push me or unplug me, and I'm fine with that. When I see bands getting mad at that happening, I ask, "Would you rather have no one at the show?" Just plug back in and play! You're here to play for people, not to get mad. I mean, it happens. A kid gets excited and unplugs you; what are you going to do? I make sure to say to the bouncers or the security: let them come up and jump off the stage, or tell them to just usher the kid off the stage. Just *please* don't go chasing them around. They're good kids, just let us handle it. You'll get respect from the fans, and that's how you run a hardcore show. We're all there for a good time and to see the band. You got beef with someone? Go outside and deal with it. I don't like that tough-guy pit nonsense. Back in the day, it was my pit antics that ultimately formed Agnostic Front. It doesn't matter if you are in the band or not, there's no reason to do that in the pit.

There's always gonna be a whole new generation of hardcore fans. When people see that you're for real, and you believe in your band, they believe in you too. You can't have a band that thinks that it's better than you. You have to embrace everyone. There's no room for beef for stupid, petty reasons. You have to be with them—meaning the fans and supporters of what you do. I get in the pit and tell jokes or hug people. I can be in the middle of a song and not have a guitar on. I'm just going for it and having a good time. You can't let success go to your head. So many bands and people, where are they now? They're gone. I mean, come to a show once in a while. Buy a record. Buy a T-shirt. You have to show up.

Over the years, I protected a lot of people at shows because I was a little older. People will tell me I stuck up for them at a show or stood by them somehow. People who were kids when they first saw Agnostic Front, now that they are grown, will come up to me and ask if I remember them. Unfortunately, I don't always remember them, but they'll tell me that I put them on my shoulders at a show we played. It was a thing

I used to do. I would put you on my shoulders and play the guitar. One time on tour, there was this little kid at one of our shows. He didn't have any tattoos, so he came on stage and we drew on him and told everyone he was Roger. My idea, of course. I really liked this kid and got such a kick out of him. At the end of the tour, we hugged, kissed, and said goodbye. He walked one way and I walked the other. He turns to me and says, "Yo, Stigma, keep it real." I said, "You want me to keep it real?! You little cocksucker, get over here! I've been keeping it real for years before you were born!"

13

Touring Musician

(Part II)

AT SOME OF OUR EARLY AGNOSTIC FRONT SHOWS, these Boston kids would come down to New York and were throwing cheap shots (on the dance floor). Basically, their hardcore thing came with a jock culture to it, rather than a street-punk culture. It wasn't cool the way they were dancing. You know when a guy is giving you a cheap shot versus just making contact while dancing. They had a little bit of a different mindset. If I were dancing alongside you and hit you when I was swinging my arms, I would apologize. When someone hits you, and you know it wasn't an accident, that's not kosher. A bunch of us wrote outside of A7, "Out of town bands, remember where you are," or something to that effect. With Agnostic Front, people were on notice. Hardcore wasn't just a weekend thing or a vacation for us.

Originally, DC and Boston had a connection together, but we, New York, seemed to be skipped over. We were like the bastard child. Years later,

Ian MacKaye would finally admit that Agnostic Front was an important band. It was like he almost didn't want to acknowledge it for a long time when it was happening. Finally, he looked back on it and said that we were a big deal.

During the early AF tours, it seems like we always had to fight, whether it was some outside force messing with us or, sometimes, even us messing with each other. We had no choice but to tour in a van in the US. We had roadies like Dave da' Skin and Frenchie in the early days. Frenchie passed away in 2001, right after 9/11. We had this show in Atlanta, Georgia. We get there, and there is this guy who apparently was the bully on the scene, who fucked up a lot of shows. I think his name was Joey Asshole. I don't know what happened, but Dave knocked him the fuck out. We heard that was the end of Joey Asshole being a bully.

There would be a few times where we would have to pull the van over so Craig (Setari) and Roger could fight for a little while. Craig is a button pusher, but I'd actually cheer for Craig. He could've beaten the shit out of Roger, but he was cool about it. Why can't we just go swimming or ride bumper cars like normal people? Instead, Agnostic Front pulls over our van so Craig and Roger can fight. Fast-forward a few years, and there'd even be beef in the airport. Steve and Mike Gallo would fight. The Gallo brothers would be yelling, screaming, choking each other, and swinging it out. I mean, look at Pete and Lou Koller: they're so quiet and nice. One's reading a book, the other's doing yoga. Steve and Mike Gallo: both are drunk, screaming and yelling. Thankfully, those days are over.

But Roger can be an asshole on the road sometimes because he's a ball breaker. It's not cool, especially on tour. That is probably the only thing that really bothers me about Roger, especially when I saw him do it to Freddy when he was little. There's no reason for that.

I remember our drummer, Joe Montanaro, and our roadie, Robert Romero, were going at it in the van. Robert was also a drummer. He works for FEMA now but has played in punk bands too. Joe and Rob started arguing about drums. We pulled the van over, set the drums up, and told them to go have a drum-off on the side of the highway. What a waste of time and energy. Who gives a fuck?!

Roger and Steve Martin were sleeping in the van one time. I was in a mood, so I went for a walk. I saw a cat and grabbed the cat from behind the neck. I opened the sliding door of the van, threw the cat in there, and quickly closed the door. The cat started freaking out from being locked in there. Roger and Steve were huddled in a corner yelling to get the cat out of there, but I was banging on the van to make the cat go nuts.

Another time, we pulled over and picked up a dead deer and took it to CBGB. That was my crazy idea. We sat on top of the deer the whole way because there was no room in the van. We brought it onto the sidewalk of CBGB and someone chopped the head off of it. Someone wound up marching around in the pit with the deer head. The police and some biohazard unit came, took the deer, and threw it in the dumpster in front of the club. I saw the legs sticking out of the dumpster, so I went over and crossed the legs. That was the same day we picked up a raccoon that had to have been about forty pounds.

Then there was the time we had a pit bull in the van. We were driving in Staten Island, and all of a sudden, the front axle just popped off the van, and we started skidding down the road. I saw it happening in slow motion. We were making a turn and were about to hit something. Then, *bang*! I don't know what we hit, but the dog went flying out the front window. It was insane! The dog was fine, in case you were wondering.

14

Touring Musician

(Part III—Europe)

IN 1990, AGNOSTIC FRONT was first invited to tour in Europe. Roger wound up being sent home as soon as we got there because of immigration issues. We called him "social garbage" jokingly, since he was a man without a country because he'd defected from Cuba. They put him on a plane and off he went back to the US. I had to carry the torch for all of us, and it was tough.

Our roadie Mike became the singer for the tour. There was always something that you couldn't trust about Mike. Allegedly, he stole the AF banner at some point. I don't know if that is true, but the guy had issues.

The tour was rough and groundbreaking at the same time. People didn't know us, really, and were calling us Nazis because of what they'd read in *Maximum RockNRoll*. We had to live that down, and I had to negotiate, fight, and have a lot of tough conversations. People are generally closed-minded. They didn't read my lyrics. Plus, it was just a rough tour. We had nothing. There was no money, no food, no place to sleep, and hardly any equipment. We just had to play the next show. I had to change one string at a time; if I broke a string, I changed just that one. It got to the point where I only had one pack of strings left.

It was like Groundhog Day every day. Every day there was someone coming up to me and challenging me. I was just trying to have a good time on tour in Europe. I mean, I would try to be polite, and tell someone to have a nice Christmas, and they would tell me they don't believe in Christmas. That's what it was like. Some people just are miserable people.

I could see if we were walking around with swastikas and saying stupid things. We weren't like that, of course. All they knew was what they'd read in that magazine. Our lyrics and our actions should have been enough. We're here and we're playing for you.

So many times the cops would come, pull us over, and put us in jail. One time, I think in Germany, I walked up to the van, and the cops were arresting everyone in the van. I'm standing behind the cops, and they don't have any clue I'm in the band. I told one of the cops to wait. I said, "I'm with them, take me along. I don't want to be out here alone." The guys were looking at me, shaking their heads. Apparently, the permit for the van was stolen or something like that. We got pulled over a bunch of times in Italy too. The guys would start fights with motorcycle gangs and white supremacist people, and then throw me out there. I had no clue what was going on. All these people would be causing trouble, saying things about us that weren't true. I was just trying to make it to the next show.

I don't know what these people wanted us to do. We play a bunch of benefits: Rock Against this, Rock Against that. What do I have to do over here? I don't want to do any fighting. I don't want to be in the middle of that.

All these assholes saw were "skinheads." C'mon, how many Black skinheads do we know? How many good skinheads are there? You can't say every skinhead is bad. That's an ignorant approach. You can't say every rapper is bad. You can't say every Chinese person, or Jew, or graffiti writer is this or that. You can't do that, because there are so many good people. But I had to fight and prove myself. I had to be vigilant and strong. I had to be positive and make friends. I knew I was paving the way. It was an uphill battle, but I was going to get to the top of that hill somehow. Then it'll be easier for the next guy.

Like I said, there was no food, no money.... We slept on a cement floor with a blanket, *and* were being ridiculed and ostracized. Of course, there were a couple of people that we made friends with, and then they made friends, and those friends made friends.

They stuck up for us, saying, "Well, Vinnie is a good guy." Believe me, I had to do a lot of negotiating—and for no reason, really. I would get mad and tell them about my grandfather during World War II. That would shut them up usually. I'd say, "Didn't my fucking grandfather come here and spill his fucking blood fighting fascism? What more do you want from my fucking family? What the fuck did

you do?" I would get really mad. I mean, my grandfather wound up with a plate in his head and half his stomach missing. He still had shrapnel in him. He got shot with a burp gun. A burp gun's like a machine gun with a tripod, and the bullet spins, it doesn't go straight. It rips you up. While he was laying there, a bomb went off. He lost half his skull and had to get a plate in his head.

A lot of bands that came after us had it much easier because we paved the way. We were hardcore punk. We were tattooed. We wore boots. We had a heavy name. We brought in a wild crowd. The younger bands wore sneakers and looked kinda suburban, so they weren't as threatening looking. But we had that stigma on us. Anyway, we did what we did and got through it. Now, Europe is incredible for Agnostic Front.

We ultimately became one of the first hardcore bands to play festivals. A lot of punk bands didn't play festivals, but somehow we got looped in. I guess it was because we took anything we could get, but we worked our asses off. Once, we were playing in France, and our drummer

at the time, Pokey, wound up in the hospital somehow. We had to grab a drummer from wherever we could; one of the other bands. I told the promoter the situation because we were high on the bill. We said we were going to try our best. The promoter told me that he started out booking Agnostic Front early on, and we had always done right by him, so we could do whatever the fuck we wanted. He asked if we needed anything else. I asked him for some ice, a.k.a. "European Diamonds." Ice isn't easy to come by in Europe. He sent us a bag of shaved ice, and the whole backstage was soaking wet. It was hilarious. Regardless, we realized that times had changed for our band.

15

Superhero

STIGMA-MAN

BY ERNIE PARADA

16

Stealer of Sleep

CRAIG SILVERMAN TAKES ALL of these pictures of me sleeping while we're on the road. Gallo takes them too sometimes. They're sneaky guys. They take photos of me asleep and post them on social media. They've got pictures of me in the van sleeping with my mouth open, sleeping backstage, sleeping on airport floors…. Everybody always asks me how I sleep so well. I don't know. I guess I can just sleep anywhere.

17

Guardian

(of the Youth)

ROGER'S LITTLE BROTHER, FREDDY, moved in with me when he was a teenager for at least a year or two. He had been living with Roger and his girlfriend, Amy, but he had a hard time getting along with Amy so they needed him to leave. I went to pick Freddy up at their place, and on the way out, she says, "Go ahead, you're going to wind up just like Vinnie Stigma, get out of here!" I swear to God, that's what she told him.

I needed to become Freddy's legal guardian, and there were a whole bunch of things I had to get done. I went to his new school to get him registered, and they told me I had to take him to a doctor to get a doctor's note so he could go to high school there and also play on the soccer team. I knew the local undertaker, who was a notary, so that was done.

Freddy Cricien (Madball): I had actually stayed with Vinnie (prior to living with him for a while) a bunch of times, but never for a really long time. A lot of people we know stayed at his place at one time or another. I'd been living on Tenth Street, sleeping in a loft bed above the bathroom, and Amy and I were butting heads. I was sixteen years old and felt like this random kid staying with their family. It became a problem, so I realized I needed to get out of there. My family trusts and loves Vinnie. I've known him since I was seven years old. He has known my mom since I

*was a kid. He's eaten at my mom's house and knows my siblings. He has
so much respect for my family, Roger especially, and I know he has a lot
of love for me.*

*He got me enrolled at Seward Park High School. I remember the
very first day walking to school with Vinnie, who was all tatted up with
a devil on his neck. Some kid got buck-fiftied at the school. The place
already looked like a jail, and there were cops everywhere and all this
chaos. Stigma's like, "What the fuck's going on in this place?" Some kid
had just gotten stabbed up, sliced open, man. It was my first day of fucking school.*

*Things settled down there eventually, and I wound up playing soccer
for the team at Seward Park. That actually kept me motivated and in
school. I'd played when I was younger and saw they had a soccer pro-
gram, so I signed up. The team was already part of the way through the
season, but the coach invited me to a practice and put me on the team. I'll
never forget seeing Stigma and Willie Shepler in the bleachers at some of
my games. That was a fuckin' trip. Vinnie was my soccer dad for a while.*

I was a soccer mom before they even invented the term. Willie and
I would be bombed on the sidelines, yelling and cheering Freddy on.
He was definitely a ball hog, and he'd throw these fits during the games.

He'd yell at the coach too and would kick the ball onto the highway and ruin the whole game. Also, when he ran, he would stick his tongue out for some reason, and we used to laugh our asses off. The whole thing was awesome.

The hardest part of living with Freddy was waking him up in the morning, because he would wake up like a fucking typhoon. He didn't want to go to school. All right, I get it, but what am I going to do? I'm responsible for him now. So I used to go over to him real quiet: "Freddy...." Shaking in my boots, because I know he's going to wake up like a fucking tyrant. But I wound up getting him to school on time somehow every day.

But man, sometimes he would get up and wreck my house. I still have holes in my wall that I cover up. One time he threw a fit because he couldn't find his passport. Roger was there for this. I had a TV on top of my refrigerator, and he picked the TV up and threw it. It went *boom*, and there was a big thing of smoke. We all got scared. Then he opened my drawers with all the knives in them, then my clothes drawers. He threw everything I owned into a pile on the floor. My whole life was in a pile on the floor in front of me. Roger and I were dying laughing.

Bottom line: I *love* Freddy! It's crazy to think he's going to be a fifty-year-old man, with a wife and kids. It's a little shocking, but then, Cubans are extremely family oriented, and also, I saw it in the lyrics he was writing about family and his friends. I was recently talking to Roger about the lyric in the Madball song "Pride (Times are Changing)": *"refuse to depend on anyone else."* Roger and I turned and looked at each other like, "Get out of here, kid." But I truly love him, and I'm very proud of who he is today.

Freddy: The man's just immensely important, not just to me, but in this whole thing we're a part of. I mean, the fact that he helped my brother, and took me under his wing; kept an eye on me and tried to keep me on the straight and narrow the best he could. Then there's the fact that without Vinnie, there's no Agnostic Front. Obviously, without AF, there's no Madball. He literally nicknamed me Madball, during one of my childhood fits of rage. He hijacked the name and was just like, "You're Madball." He christened me. Roger's had a huge part in it, obviously, but Vinnie's equally responsible for me doing what I do for a living and who I've become. He's just super important and has been instrumental in so much.

18

Hotel

MY PLACE HAS ALWAYS BEEN Agnostic Front headquarters, New York Hardcore headquarters really. Because I had my whole family here, there was always food here; I had an address, a landline, an answering machine, a shower, and a place for people to sleep. Plus, I make friends easily. For instance, in '84, '85, when we had the New York/Montreal Connection, where we had all the bands from Canada come down to play, they all stayed  here, four bands in this apartment. People had to be like, "Excuse me," stepping over everyone sleeping on the floor. We would take towels and cut them into pieces so everybody would have their own. It was chaos, but I enjoyed having them here. Back then, none of the bands got hotels, so I felt like I was helping out, doing whatever I could. Whoever needed a place to stay, this was the place.

So many people stayed here at one time or another: Paul Bearer, Harley, John Watson, Hoya, Bundy.... Of course Roger and Freddy. Steve Poss used to stay here when I would go away. My mother loved him. He was the little Jewish boy she always wanted. I was like, you should only know. The list goes on. I remember when Todd Youth was eleven years old, he used to run away from his home and come stay with me. I would call his mother to let her know he was at my house. I would ask her if she fed him, because he always looked like he was starving. Anyone who was ever in the band: Matty Henderson lived with me, Will Shepler lived here, a lot of people. I didn't mind it at all. It was an experience. Plus, if I didn't like you, I'd just throw you out.

People truly appreciated the hospitality. I didn't ask for anything in return. But, say, if I needed a container of milk, I'd send them to go get the container of milk, but I'd cook for them. I'd make eggs in the morning or whatever. That was the easiest and cheapest thing, especially when I was hosting bands. Rancid came here, Lars's band, but they really just needed the shower and a place to chill out, and to leave their stuff somewhere secure. So I always had a place like that. Sometimes, when we had the Black and Blue Bowl, in the early days, everybody would leave their bags at my tattoo shop. If you needed something, I was there to help.

19

Solo Artist

(Stigma, the Band)

You know, Hatebreed was the only "big" band to ever take Agnostic Front on the road. Over the years, so many of them told us they wanted to, or were going to, but none of them did, not for an entire tour. There was Pantera, Slayer, Anthrax…. The Dropkick Murphys did actually return the favor of having them play with us a lot. We helped Al's band The Bruisers too, but honestly, Hatebreed was the only one. One time I asked Jamey (Jasta) why he was so good to Agnostic Front. He  told me, "Vinnie, when I was seventeen, you bought me a birthday cake, and I'll never forget that." I remembered we had played at his party, and I brought him a cake. I got it at Venieros over on Eleventh Street.

He and I would pal around in the studio, or on their bus, or back-stage, or whatever, and one day he says to me, "Stigma, it's time for you to do a solo record." I had been in Agnostic Front for over twenty-five years, and Roger had gone solo, so I figured I could throw a solo record together. But it's all Jamey's fault! He even helped me write the Stigma *New York Blood* record.

Again, it had been like a quarter century with the band, so I decided I wasn't going to play guitar in this band. I wanted to do something totally different. It's not Agnostic Front. We're a good-time-Charlie band; you know, everybody loves us. They know who we are. They know what to expect. I've got great musicians on the record, great writing, great songs. People tell me, "Vinnie, just watching you guys, I had a great time." It's good party music. Sometimes I bring a rolling bar out there, and I have this thing where I yell at the band. I end the song, and then they end it late. I'm like, "Hey, you want to stop the damn song?! These fucking guys." We just have fun. I involve the audience too. You have to.

I'd like to do more with Stigma, but my band doesn't want to do it, because one guy's in another band, this guy's moving away.... Other guys have come up to me and said, "Yo, we'll learn ten songs and record or play a show." So I'm like, "Fuck it. Fuck these guys. We'll write the fucking ten songs." I want to do something on the weekends, you know what I mean? They're free nights out for me. I want to go out, drink, smoke a little weed, hang out, and entertain people. That's what I do.

20

Dad

I HAVE A SON, VINCENT III. He is an adult now, and a true American. He is part Asian. His mother and I have never gotten married but are still together. I met her at a Napalm Death/Obituary show, where she was with a couple of friends, and I offered to introduce her to the band. That's how we started talking. I asked her out on a date and we met up at Tower Records. About a year or so into our relationship, we were expecting Vincent. Our focus was getting our life together and having our son. The rest is history.

Once we found out we were having a boy, I wanted his name to be Vincent to continue my family tradition beginning with my father. My son has a giant family: some blood, and many others, friends who've become family. We had a lot of his birthday parties at the house, and all his uncles would be there. We'd eat, get drunk, and celebrate my kid's birthday. Jimmy from Murphy's Law is his godfather, and Paula Reinhardt

is his godmother. He's always had
hardcore uncles and aunts, kind of
how we all became Freddy's uncles
when he was little. Now Freddy is
an uncle to my son.

I love all the different types
of people and influences he has
around him. I remember one day
when Vincent was five or so, he was
playing in the park, and Hoya and
I were sitting there watching him
play. He came up to me and asked
if it was okay that he liked brown
people. I was dumbfounded. I told him of course it was alright. Look at
Uncle Hoya. Hoya told him to simply judge people for who they are, not
to worry, and to try to like everyone. I can't imagine where he picked up
the idea that it might not be okay to like other people based on race. He's
bi-racial himself, so it's odd that my kid would ask that. I take it seriously
that it is my job, and every parent's job, to teach children decency.

Vincent and I have gone to a lot of baseball games. One time we went
to a Yankees game, and he thought it would be funny to run away into
the crowd and hide to scare me. I got all crazy, and he would laugh at me
because he thought it was hilarious. He was a little bit of a prankster. We
went to a few hockey games, too, saw some bull riding, and we'd play ball
in the yard. We would also do karate together at a place Paula taught at.
Paula is a personal bodyguard for rich women, because some of them
feel more comfortable with a woman protecting them.

Vincent doesn't have much interest in playing music, but he does like
some music. He likes H2O but isn't into Agnostic Front. He likes the
more melodic type stuff. I wish he were more into it and had an interest
in the guitar, but I can't force that on him. He is more into tech. He's a
gamer and computer kid with a room full of screens. All I see is the back

of his head while he plays his games. I'll ask him if we can talk, and he turns around and asks me, "Well, what do you want to talk about?" then just goes back to his games. That's how kids are today.

I'm just trying to be the best dad I can be. I provide as best I can, but you will never have enough money, your house will never be big enough, and you'll never have the best car. You want it. You strive for it, but it's always a struggle. As our parents used to say, at least we have our health.

Vincent III: He was always there for me when I was a kid. He was around and took care of me with my mom. Maybe he was off on tours and whatnot a lot, but it was nice to hang around with him when he was home. He was just supportive. He can be a pain, especially with how he is sometimes, but my parents, they love each other very much, even if they kind of butt heads or get annoyed with each other sometimes.

I really like that he's out there making music for people to enjoy, and enjoy himself. He gets to hang out with his friends: adventuring, meeting new people, and making good music. I'm proud of what he does, especially seeing him up on stage. I do hope one day I can find something that will inspire me, or grab my genuine interest the way music has with my dad.

I only learned about hardcore from him taking me to his concerts to show me off to his friends, like, "Hey, here's my son." I've never gotten to go on any tours with him though.

I tried to learn how to play the guitar once, but that was when I was in middle school. I haven't played it for many years now, but I still remember when he got me the guitar, which now is in my room in a box.

He's always asking me if I'm doing all right. He'll ask if I need money. He always tries to encourage me to do my best and gives me that bit of push to be sure I'm doing well for myself. He's just a good guy and a good dad, and it's nice knowing that he is kind of this big-shot musician in a band playing for lots of people who just really enjoy his music.

21

Cancer Survivor

WHEN I WAS FIFTY, let's just say…I started leaking oil. I was touring a lot with Hatebreed at the time, and they all used to make fun of me because my underwear would become soiled. Like, when I'd be sleeping, they'd be taking pictures of my underwear. Anyway, whatever. I knew there was a problem.

I went ahead and unionized my tattoo shop—if you know what I mean—for the health coverage. That tattoo shop saved my life. If I didn't have the tattoo shop, I wouldn't have had health insurance and wouldn't have gone to the doctor.

I said to myself, "Fuck it, I have to go." I went to my guy Dr. Dave, because I didn't want to go to a stranger. I felt comfortable with him. Nowadays, I don't care. I'll go in front of the Macy's window and pull my pants down. At this point, I just want to make people aware. So I went to Dr. Dave, who is my primary care doctor. He did an EKG, piss test, X-rays, blood work, and all that stuff. Then, he sent me to this little Arab guy, who was more of a specialist.

He gave me a colonoscopy and afterward tells me that I have fistula tumors growing on my colon and that I needed colorectal surgery. He said, "If we don't get it now, you might have to wear a colostomy bag for the rest of your life." I said, "Whoa, then let's go right now. Take me down the hall. Let's do it today." So that spooked me a little, but it changed my fucking tune real quick. Of course plenty of people had it worse than I did, but I was basically just told I had cancer.

While I was at the appointment with the specialist, he says to me, "I hear you're some kind of rock star or something, you play music." I told him I wasn't a rock star, but was in kind of a popular band and played guitar, and that I had records out. I brought him a CD the next time I saw him for the surgery. The surgery seemed to go fine, but after a bit of time, he told me I had to have a second operation because they may not have gotten it all.

So, I go back for a second surgery, and they cleaned everything out. I remember them giving me an epidural with a needle the size of my fucking leg. When they put the needle in, I jumped off the table because I felt the whole thing. The surgeon said, "I guess we should give him some more anesthesia." Yeah, good idea.

When I woke up, I asked the doctor if he ever listened to the CD I gave him. He said, "Yeah, we just listened to it while we were operating." I was like, "You listened to that garbage while I was on the table?! You're supposed to be listening to Beethoven or Mozart!" We laughed and it was all cool. I go back in for check-ups, but they gave me a clean bill of health. I'm very lucky.

22

Culinary School Dropout

I MET A LOT OF PEOPLE at Max's Kansas City, whether it was members of The Stilettos, which had Debbie Harry and Chris Stein from Blondie in there, or Buddy Bowser, who was the sax player for the New York Dolls, or Richard Hell. I bought a studio over on Varick Street from Richard Hell and was actually living there for a while. A few floors up was the New York Culinary Academy. I eventually lost the studio, but I liked cooking and was curious about the Culinary Academy. I decided to check it out and went for around two weeks. I wound up feeling like, "This ain't for me. I can't afford it, and I just don't care. I got a grand-mother who'll teach me that stuff. I don't need these fucking guys," so I quit.

I did learn a few things, though. There are a bunch of stages and levels they make you go through. They start you in produce, learning about all of the different vegetables. Then meats. Plus, you have to learn about refrigeration. No one wants meat with freezer burn; it tastes like chalk. I had done air conditioning and refrigeration before, so I understood it a little. You had to learn the flame levels, the different pots and pans, cooking with oil and butter.... It was a long time ago, and I really couldn't put all my eggs in that basket, so to speak. You know, every Italian guy thinks he knows how to cook. It's just a thing.

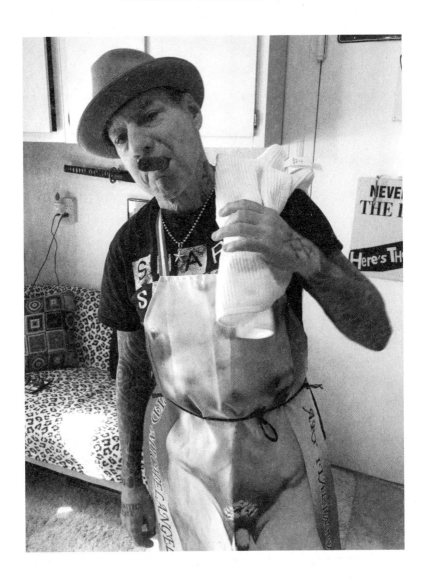

23

Cook

It may surprise people, but I'm a little bit of a cook, mostly stovetop cooking, not a lot of baking. I got my interest in cooking from all the old ladies in my building when I was a kid. There was my grandmother, my mother, my aunts, and a few of the others who had their little specialties. I was like their sous-chef: opening the cans, getting the pans from the top shelf, keeping an eye on the flame, peeling the garlic....

If you think about it, Italian food has it all: vegan, vegetarian, whatever. Do you want to eat vegan? No problem. You want the food to be gluten free? Not a problem. Italians don't think about making food to fit into this category or that category. It's just food.

I enjoy doing the old-school dishes. My recipes are simple. Everybody can look at them and say, "Oh, I can do that." They're great for when I come home from tour or just a late night out. They are also perfect if you're in college, living in a dorm somewhere on a budget. They're quick, easy, and don't need a lot of ingredients. We all have to eat, so you might as well learn. I always say, "If you are able to cook for one, you can cook for two. If you can cook for two, you can cook for four. You cook for four, you could cook for an army." I learned that from my mother. So, what's the difference? You have to cook anyway. Of course, they are great anytime. You're not going to cook for hours in the middle of the night, so these are easy and also cheap. They're what are called "peasant dishes." They were originally put together by relatively poor people

and only needed what families generally always had in their kitchens. Every culture has their version(s) of peasant dishes. The ingredients aren't hard to find.

I've been cooking since I was twelve years old when I was a line cook at Ballato's around the corner from my house. I did a bunch of stuff there. I swept the floors, set the tables, and washed dishes. Mr. Ballato used to give me a little bit of money. He was a big-time chef. My mother knows all his recipes, including clams oreganata, but I'm not doing that. I hate cooking fish. But any of my recipes, you can throw some shrimp or chicken in there easily. At the end, just sprinkle some pecorino Romano cheese on it, and boom!

Of course you're gonna need some olive oil. You can get very expensive olive oil if you want, but it can be the cheaper stuff too. I remember one time, I had a forty-dollar bottle of imported Colavita olive oil, which is one of the pricier olive oils. Gallo and Ezec used my olive oil to make macaroni and cheese. Then they threw my Gorgonzola cheese away because they thought it was rotten. They said it stunk and was all moldy. That was about fifty dollars' worth of cheese they threw away. They also drank my cooking wine. I said, "You guys are animals!" I came home to a culinary nightmare. That olive oil was to drizzle over mozzarella and tomatoes Caprese. These guys were cooking with it. They drank my white wine, and they drank my red wines that I cook with. I wanted to choke the two of them!

Anyway, I love to cook. I do it for friends and I cook for myself. Check out my little Neapolitan recipes:

STIGMA MARINARA

Ingredients
1 (15 oz.) can of crushed tomatoes
2 tbsp. of olive oil
2 cloves of garlic, sliced
Red pepper flakes (to Taste)

For a simple marinara sauce, get a can of crushed tomatoes. Get your garlic sauteed in your oil, and add your red pepper flakes. Add a little water, because the crushed tomatoes are very thick and concentrated. Rinse the tomato can out, and add the water to your pot. You have to keep the cover on it and stir it as you go. In about 30 minutes, you got your sauce. This is just a quick, go-to sauce that's easy to cook. While that is cooking, make your pasta of choice. Finish your dish off with some cheese. My preference is pecorino Romano cheese. If I was asked what my pasta of choice was for the marinara sauce, I would say capellini. It's a thin angel-hair pasta, but you can also use ziti, which is always easy to find.

STIGMA BOLOGNESE

Same as the marinara sauce, but you throw some meat in there. About 20 minutes before the marinara is done, add cooked and drained ground meat. Gotta drain the meat ahead of time because it has a lot of oil.

PASTA FAZOOL, a.k.a. PASTA E FAGIOLI

Ingredients

3–4 tbsp. of olive oil, approximately
2 cloves of garlic, sliced
Red pepper flakes (to Taste)
1 (15.5 oz.) can of cannellini beans
1 (8 oz.) can of tomato sauce (for red version)
8 oz. of stock, chicken or vegetable (for white version)
4 servings of small pasta shells
Salt (to taste)
Pepper (to taste)
Basil (to taste)

Back in the day, you would take the beans you use in this recipe and soak them for a day or two. I don't do that. I use the cannellini beans out of a can. As is the norm with Italian dishes, first you sauté sliced garlic in some olive oil. I use 2 cloves, but you can always use as much or as little as you like. Add a few shakes of red pepper flakes to the oil. Once you have the garlic and red pepper flakes sautéed, you add the can of cannellini beans. Now there are two ways you can make the dish: either red or white. If you want to make it red, add a little can of tomato sauce in there. If you want to make the white version of pasta *e fagioli*, it's the same process, except instead of using tomato sauce, you use some chicken or vegetable stock. I prefer it with the chicken stock, because to me, it just tastes better and is more traditional. Then add some salt, pepper, and basil to taste. Keep the flame to a nice low flame and simmer it for about an hour. I like to simmer my dishes for an hour, because when the bean is nice and soft, the flavor really comes out. By the way, most Italians don't measure anything. We just taste it along the way. If you need more seasoning, you throw in a pinch of this, or a pinch of that.

Next comes the macaroni. I boil up some small shells, but you could use almost any pasta. Remember, this is a peasant dish. People used whatever they had in their house. When everything is done cooking, I combine the macaroni and the sauce and beans. Then I clean out the can the beans were in, and fill it with some of the pasta water to pour into the dish to make it more of a soup. You can make it thicker too, but I like it more like a soup.

PASTA BASILE, a.k.a. PASTA WITH TOMATO AND BASIL

Ingredients

1 tsp. of olive oil
1 small onion, chopped
    (approximately ½ cup)
1 (8 oz.) can of tomato sauce
4 servings of medium pasta shells
    or penne pasta
Red pepper flakes (to taste)
Salt (to taste)
Pepper (to taste)
Dried basil (to taste)

For this dish you take a teaspoon of oil and some chopped onion and sauté it in a pot. Add some red pepper flakes, then you add the red sauce. This dish only goes with red sauce. The same little can of, say, Del Monte tomato sauce. Add some salt and pepper to taste, and then the basil. I like to use dried basil because it has a long shelf life. If you buy the fresh, you have to use it right away because it dries out two days later. My pasta of choice is medium shells. If you can't find those, you can use the small penne pasta. My mother used to break up spaghetti and throw it in. Sometimes if all I have is some ziti, I throw it in. This is another peasant dish. Use a little bit of the pasta water to find the consistency you like. If you want it to have a soup consistency, add more pasta water. If you like it thicker, only add a little. I prefer it to be thick.

PASTA CHEE CHEE, a.k.a. PASTA E CECI

Ingredients

1 tsp. of olive oil
2 cloves of garlic, sliced
1 (8 oz.) can of tomato sauce or crushed/peeled tomatoes
    (for red version)
8 oz. of stock, chicken or vegetable (for white version)
4 servings of your pasta of choice
1 (15 oz.) can of chickpeas
Red pepper flakes (to taste)
Salt (to taste)
Pepper (to taste)

Another dish is called pasta e ceci, a.k.a. pasta with chickpeas. Once again, we start the dish the same way: oil, garlic, and red pepper flakes. You throw a can of chickpeas in. For those who don't know what chickpeas are, they are garbanzo beans. This dish you can also make red with tomato sauce or crushed and peeled tomatoes, or white by adding chicken or vegetable stock. Add salt, pepper, and basil to taste. Sometimes I used crushed tomatoes—the peeled, crushed plum tomatoes. Add it to the pasta, and you got it.

PASTA PRIMAVERA

Ingredients

1 tsp. of olive oil
2 cloves of garlic, sliced
1 cup of cherry or grape tomatoes
1 cup vegetable of choice, chopped (zucchini, broccoli, peppers,
    carrots...)
4 servings of your pasta of choice
Red pepper flakes (to taste)
Salt (to taste)
Pepper (to taste)
4 servings of your pasta of choice

Now we've got pasta primavera. When I make it, I use the little cherry tomatoes, but you can use grape tomatoes too. As with the other dishes, you start off with the oil, garlic, and red pepper flakes, just enough to coat the bottom of your pot. For this dish, I keep the garlic a little more solid. I don't slice it as thin. Since this dish has chunks of vegetables in it, you use zucchini—or really, anything—but chop it up. Throw that in the pot along with your tomatoes. Everything goes in the pot together. Add a little bit more oil to coat all your vegetables but you don't want them swimming in oil. Make your pasta of choice and you're done.

RAPINI, a.k.a. BROCCOLI RABE

Ingredients

1 tsp. of olive oil
2 cloves of garlic, sliced
1 large bunch of broccolini (or 1 large head of regular broccoli)
Red pepper flakes (to taste)
Salt (to taste)
Pepper (to taste)

One of my favorite things is broccolo, or broccoli rabe. I heat up my oil, garlic, and red pepper flakes in a pot. Sometimes I cut the broccolo up into smaller parts just for consistency. You can buy a bunch of it at the store. Wash it off and cut it up. Everyone has their own way of using it. Add your salt and pepper. You can steam the broccolo for about 20 minutes with the oil and the garlic. Then you're done. It's totally delicious. I usually toast up a piece of bastone (Italian bread) or a baguette. I add some Gorgonzola cheese on top, then the broccolo. There's two kinds of Gorgonzola. One is more blue and it's a little harder. The other one, the one I like to use, is the creamier one.

I cook spinach the same way. Oil, garlic, and red pepper flakes. I usually use frozen spinach. Maybe add some salt to finish it off. It's the most delicious spinach when you have a pile of it. I like to use frozen because you can keep it for whenever you need it. Fresh is good, too, if that is your preference, but you have to use it right away.

FETTUCCINE ALFREDO

Ingredients

2 egg yolks
8 oz. of heavy cream
3–4 tbsp. of butter
2 servings of fettuccine egg noodles
Red pepper flakes (to taste)
Salt (to taste)
Pepper (to taste)

Another recipe I put together is a fettuccine Alfredo. This dish uses heavy cream and egg yolks. For two people, I would use 2 egg yolks, no egg whites. Add some black pepper. Mix that up and get it to where it is room temperature. Boil your fettuccine egg noodles in salted water. When you drain it, keep the noodles a little wet. Add them back to their pot, and throw in some butter (maybe a third of a stick or half a stick) along with the heavy cream and egg yolks. Add some red pepper flakes and some pepper and that's it. Sometimes people may want it a little more yellow (more yolks) or more creamy (heavy cream/butter). If that's the case, just make sure it is room temperature before adding it to the pasta so it doesn't shock it. At the end before eating, I sprinkle some Locatelli cheese over it.

CANNOLI

I'm not a baker, so if I want a ganool, a.k.a. cannoli, I just go down-stairs to the cafe and get one. I can't make them for my life! And you can't let them sit around too long, because the shells get soft. Have some coffee with that, and you'll be happy. I drink coffee all the time. I can even drink it at night and go right to sleep. I have a little Italian moka pot, or sometimes I do the French press. I like Medaglia d'Oro coffee in my moka pot, but sometimes, for a change of pace, or if I'm feeling lazy, I'll just go buy a cup from a coffee shop.

24

Friend to Vegans

You want to know something about vegans? Oh, don't worry... they'll tell you!

25

Dancer

MOSHING: SOME PEOPLE SAY I (accidentally) invented the term, but I don't know if that's true or not. I do say it a lot, though. I know the Bad Brains, when they got heavy into the Rasta thing, used to say "MASH it up" or "MASH up the place," like a lot of reggae bands would say. Supposedly, I was yelling out what H.R. said on stage, but my accent made it sound like "MOSH" instead of "MASH," and it went on from there. Now everyone is MOSHing!

Back at Max's Kansas City and early on at CBGB, they did the pogoing and slam dancing stuff. There was no real style to it, just people jumping up and down, bashing into one another. The moshing thing came later; that creepy-crawl, get-down-low-to-the-slower-parts New

York style. I mean, we had small clubs in New York like A7. There was no room to do a circle pit.

I was always a friendly mosher. I never would step on your foot or kick you just to be a jerk. Never like, "I want to be the hardest one out here." We're all here having fun. Your band goes up to play your songs, I'll mosh to your band. Then I get up there, and you mosh to my band. We'll all have fun together. I jump on you, you jump on me. Fun chaos.

We used to do all kinds of stupid things in the pit. The scratch, as if I had an itch. The pizza maker. Picking up change. I used to do the dirty bird. Then there were the chicken fights. You just had to free yourself. Everybody knew you were just having fun, and people would bring their own style to it.

Now, there's the whole karate thing going on. It's a different head, but I get it. Then there are guys nowadays that ruin the pit by doing something called "crowd killing." It's where people are basically running amok on the dance floor just punching people. That doesn't happen in New York. People would never get away with that bullshit here, but I've seen it at shows in other places. People just run up and punch people in the face. What the fuck is that about?! I guess the music has changed, so the dancing style changed. The attitude is different. And it's funny, because now it's the metal kids who are doing the circle pits. Lately, Roger likes to throw me down into the crowd with my guitar, and we get the crowd to circle pit around me. I guess I'm helping to preserve the circle pit. I'm the monkey in the middle over here.

26

Wrestler

I was a big wrestling fan as a kid and watched it every Saturday after the cartoons. My favorite wrestler, of course, was Bruno Sammartino, the living legend. I saw him up close once. The guy was like a refrigerator: a thick, naturally built specimen. They don't make guys like that no more. I liked Superstar Billy Graham, André the Giant, Superfly Jimmy Snuka…and who didn't love Lou Albano? But Bruno Sammartino was my favorite. He was against steroids and all that. He had been a Greco-Roman wrestler, like a real wrestler before WWF. It's just incredible entertainment.

I've always fantasized about being a wrestler, and I finally got to live out my wrestling fantasy recently. Our friend, Kevin Gill, who used to

have a little hardcore record label, is a big wrestling announcer now. He's great. He says to me, "Do you like wrestling? Do you want to wrestle one day?" I'm like, "Yeah, sure, I'll want to do it." So he eventually called, and I did it. I did it twice actually, and I know I did a good job.

Kevin Gill (the Voice of Independent Wrestling): I am a pro wrestling commentator and ring announcer, currently working with Outlaw Wrestling in New York, Circle 6 in Los Angeles, as well as Middle Kingdom Wrestling in Shanghai. I have been a fan of Vinnie and Agnostic Front for many years. A few years ago, we talked about his desire to do stuff in wrestling outside of his legendary brawl with WWE Hall of Famer "Luscious" Johnny Valiant. I always had it in my mind but I was trying to think which wrestling promotion would make the most sense to feature him.

When I moved back to New York, I was hanging out with Stigma at a show and posted a photo of the two of us on Instagram. My buddy, pro wrestler Bull James, saw the post, called me up, and asked me if I thought Vinnie would ever want to do something with Outlaw Wrestling in New York City. Bull is a guy I have known and trusted for a long time, so I knew having a 6' 3" three-hundred-pound wrestler watching Vinnie's back made me even more comfortable with the idea. I said, "Funny you should mention that…Vinnie is really interested in getting involved in wrestling, and Outlaw being in New York makes it the perfect location."

The next thing I did was call Craig Ahead from Sick of It All and told him what we were planning. The moment I mentioned Stigma and wrestling, Craig was just like, "Oh my god! You have to do this, Gilly. Stigma was made for this!" My talk with Craig added a confidence boost going into my call with Vinnie.

I contacted Vinnie and told him we had the idea for him to manage quintessential NYC wrestler and worldwide phenomenon Homicide in his huge Outlaw Championship match against former ECW and WCW star Crowbar in a Dog Collar Match at the Queens Brewery. Vinnie was all about it instantly. He was so excited about the opportunity and you could feel the energy in his voice. He was also very grateful for the opportunity to do his thing and thanked me profusely. It felt really good to be able to give something back to a man who's given so much to us with his music and the living example he has set for all of us in hardcore.

I walked him through the idea of managing Homicide and told him that we would connect them at the show so they could get a feel for each other and figure out the best stuff that could be done. He was totally down!

Needless to say, Vinnie fit into the locker room like a respected and decorated veteran of the sport. Sometimes special guests from outside of wrestling can rub certain performers the wrong way, and you kinda have to run interference or steer certain people away. That was not the case with Stigma. Vinnie interacted with everyone performing on the show: watched everyone's matches, talked to them about their matches, showed up early and stayed late like a true student of the game. He wanted to do as much as possible to add to the impact of the main event, the Dog Collar Match. His excitement and passion was infectious and brought a magic and manic energy to the proceedings. It felt surreal to look into the crowd and see so many notable New York hardcore folks losing their minds when Stigma entered the ringside area. There were also several wrestlers on the show, as well as people on the production crew and venue staff who were huge Agnostic Front fans, who, as we say in wrestling, "marked out" and took photos with Vinnie backstage.

EVENT 1—Vinnie arrived at the building earlier than call time and we hung out a bit. I introduced him to everyone as they came in and before long, Homicide arrived. Once the pleasantries and small talk were done, Bull James came over and started throwing around some ideas with Vinnie and Homicide to break the ice and get things rolling. It didn't take much, as Stigma and Homicide were off to the races discussing the possibilities, laughing and joking like old friends. I knew some stuff Vinnie was going to do, but not all of it. It was absolutely insane to me, as well as to the fans in attendance, to see Vinnie play such a pivotal and hands-on role in the match. At one point, he climbed the ropes and soared through the air fearlessly before colliding with and taking down his target. Vinnie rallied the crowd behind Homicide and was not at all *afraid of getting physical. When all was said and done, with Vinnie in his corner, Homicide was able to defeat Crowbar for the Outlaw Wrestling Championship on this fateful night. Vinnie and Homicide celebrated this monumental win with the fans, as (his song) "New York Blood" blared through the PA before Vinnie and Homicide made their closing remarks. From the moment he came out to his music, to the moment the main event concluded, Vinnie was an absolute natural and killed it. It was funny, because I am always nervous about travel and scheduling issues before a show and I said to Craig the night before the show, "I just hope Vinnie shows up." Without missing a beat, Craig replied, "You wouldn't be able to stop him from showing up," and he was right!*

EVENT 2—Vinnie was such a hit in his inaugural performance, he was quickly invited back to Outlaw Wrestling NYC and was made the commissioner of the league for his second appearance, so we amended the commissioner title to be "The Commissioner of Chaos." During his second night in Outlaw, shit got out of control with "The Samoan Storm" Afa Anoa'i Junior—the son of WWE Hall of Famer Afa the Wild Samoan—and Samoan Dynasty member Jacob Fatu (both of whom are from the same famous wrestling family/bloodline as The Rock, Roman Reigns, Jimmy and Jey Uso, Rikishi, Umaga, just to name a few) attacking wrestlers during the show. At one point, Jacob Fatu and Afa Junior cornered Vinnie Stigma in the ring and were about to get physical with him, so Bull James and Homicide rushed the ring and cleaned house.

I stood in the darkened area where the wrestlers enter the ringside area with Vinnie as we waited for our cue and talked about the interview segment. Vinnie came to the ring as animatedly and charismatically as he performs on stage and announced that he was now the Commissioner of Chaos for Outlaw Wrestling and would not tolerate any bullshit. He received a hero's welcome and ultimately ordered the main event: Homicide and Bull James versus Jacob Fatu and Afa Anoa'i Junior.

At the end of the night, neither Stigma nor the referee could contain the chaos, and the main event ended in a no contest. Ever the showman, Vinnie grabbed the mic and sang live vocals to "New York Blood"

along with the crowd, as the hardcore anthem once again blazed through the sound system at the Queens Brewery. Mr. Goombah sent them home happy.

The original idea was that I would be the manager, kinda like Lou Albano, but that plan changed. I came in as a manager, but wound up getting beat up, getting involved. I even came off the top rope. I was thinking, I can do that because of CBGB. I know how to stage dive. One fat guy throws me into the *other* fat guy. Then *that* fat guy throws me to *another* fat guy. I'm only like 147 pounds, so a big fat guy can throw me around. I climbed up the ropes and launched myself. It was incredible. My friend took his wife. She didn't want to go—you know, "I don't like wrestling. It's stupid." She wound up saying, "I can't wait for the next one!" She was biting down on her hand. That's how much she was loving it. Oh my God!

Afterward, I was like. "Holy shit! I just lived out my fantasy." I flew off the top ropes. I fought famous guys who were in the ring with me, and we won the belt that night. That was the clincher right there. I got the belt. And then, I went and did it again.

I fought some of the Wild Samoans' kids. They were on a wrestling tour, so they stopped off at this event, just like a band. They had the hair, the big Samoan bodies…they wore those lavalavas, the Samoan shorts, they had the tribal tattoos…. Just like the first time, they'd pick me up, throw me; one fat guy threw me to the other fat guy. We planned it out backstage, but I told them, "Remember, don't talk to me when we're out there." We've got to be enemies. I was giving them dirty looks, trying not to laugh.

Of course, I had a great wrestling name: "Stigma the Magnificent!" My managerial name was "Mr. Goombah." I probably need to come out on stage with Agnostic Front wearing a cape, which is something I've actually done before.

Kevin Gill: In my original call with Vinnie, he asked respectfully if I would hear "an idea or two" that he had and I said, "Of course." He then unleashed a totally in-depth character synopsis of "Mr. Goombah" and the things he would say and do. Not just one or two things, but tons of hilariously perfect ideas and explorations of the character, and all the big-picture and subtle details of Mr. Goombah. It was incredible. Vinnie put more thought into his character than many professionals who have been in the business for years had done. "Stigma the Magnificent," to my knowledge, is another one of those Stigma creations. Vinnie does not just create riffs, songs, unity, and brotherhood. He also can create characters and concepts from formation to execution and performance. His love and passion for wrestling is deep, and the respect he has for the artform and those who sacrifice their bodies to entertain, goes back a long, long way.

I loved every second of it. I even have plans to hold a children's day at wrestling, and at the end, have all the kids beat me up. I would try to grab all the kids, but they'll always get away. I'd just miss them, and chase them all out of the ring, and have all the little kids cry. I can't wait to pull that off.

27

Actor

New York Blood film description from IMDb:

Drug dealing mobster Vinnie (Vinnie Stigma), who owns a neighborhood whorehouse, wants to take care of his father, Lorenzo (Marvin W. Schwartz), a convicted murderer just released from prison.

My friend Nicky the Knife from Pittsburgh is a film guy and wanted to make a movie with me in it. I said, "Okay, let's do this." We did a thing called "Gangster Gore." It wasn't a real mafia movie, and it wasn't a real gore movie. But I couldn't get fucking anybody to come help me with

the movie. Thank God I had (Mike) Gallo, but I had to beg people to be in it, like, "Somebody come help me out over here." Even if you can just walk by me, be an extra, like, "Yeah…what are you looking at?" Just case the scene.

Everybody thinks about being an actor at some point. I mean, Frank Sinatra…. I wanted to do it, but it wasn't a dream or anything like that. Wrestling was a dream, but I figured, if Frank can do it, so could I. Plus, I've made a bunch of music videos before and have been in front of the camera, so I figured, "Fuck it." You're acting in those videos anyway, you know, "Walk from here to here," or whatever.

Then there's *Dick Dynamite:1944*, which I'm in. You've got Nazis, you've got zombies, UFOs, you've got fast cars. You've got more killing than all the *Terminator* movies put together. It's over the top, like *Sharknado* or *Cocaine Bear*. It's kinda like, "Who the hell thought of this?" But it's fun.

28

Canvas

My tattoos are somewhat traditional. I have a mix of Japanese tattoos, Italian tattoos, and memorial tattoos. I never got the Jesus heads or the panther tattoos like the old *Cugini* (Italian for cousins) in Brooklyn.

There were people in my family who were tattooed. All my cousins got panthers, and I have a cousin whose Jesus tattoo looks a little too much like Rocky Balboa. My uncles had all been tattooed by Charlie Wagner. He was on the Bowery, and they pretty much got tattooed for a bottle of wine and ten cents. Charlie was a well-known tattoo artist, and his signature was these little stars that he used to throw around the tattoos. So my uncles got them after World War II, and that was my first kind of influence as far as tattoos go. There was also this guy named Alley Cat in my neighborhood, who was a sailor. Later on, I was one of the first guys to get tattooed on the New York scene. I mean, tattoos go back thousands of years, but early on, I was considered to be pretty heavily tattooed, even though if you had maybe four tattoos, you were considered to be heavily tattooed back in the day.

I got my first tattoo in 1971. It was from a guy uptown, Sailor Dave, and he had this apprentice, Mickey. He was a Puerto Rican kid in Spanish Harlem and tattooed in his apartment. Everyone in New York tattooed in an apartment back then because it was illegal. I looked at his flash on the wall, and I pointed and said, "I want that one." I think it was twenty bucks. They were all maybe fifteen or twenty dollars. It was one needle for everybody, no gloves, nothing, and everyone there smoked and drank. Lots of alcoholics and drug addicts around. I also got tattooed early on by Thom deVita and a guy named Freddy who worked for Thom right here on the Lower East Side. Lots of Italian guys from the neighborhood would get a Jesus tattoo, or a holy cross, or "Mom" inside the banner. To think, now you got straight-edge guys doing vegan tattooing. I'm like, "Who the

fuck wants to get tattooed by this fuck!?" Tattoos are supposed to be more of an outlaw thing.

But I like the original flash art. I like traditional: American and Japanese. People brought that stuff back to America from the wars. It was an honorable thing, and there was a different mindset. There were a lot of guys running around the neighborhood who had that one tattoo, like a big dragon or an eagle or something. Tough guys. If you were a tough guy, you got a tattoo. Around '73, '74, I got a thundercloud done on my chest up in Harlem. I was getting tattooed in one room and out of nowhere I hear *bang! bang!* They came up and shot someone in the next room. I'm pretty sure it was the tattoo guy's wife. I was like, "Fuck this," and I ran out the window, no shirt on, in the middle of Harlem. I ran down the fire escape from the fifth floor. I had no idea where I was or where I was going. I just jumped on the nearest downtown train with no shirt on and went home with half a tattoo, bleeding from my chest.

I think Agnostic Front was the first American band to be fully tattooed, with shaved heads, that toured the United States. When people saw us, they were like, *Wow, who are these guys?!* They didn't know if we were bikers, or this, or that, but they knew we were something a little different. And if you know me, you know I just go make friends with everybody, so I kind of brought it around to people. Obviously, there were no tattoo magazines yet, so us bringing it out there on the road across the country was important. Later on, we took it to Europe and other places.

In the early days of AF, Elio Espana started tattooing us at my apartment. We were kind of his guinea pigs, but we wanted tattoos. He was also teaching us about tattooing. Because I lived so close to CBGB, people would come over here when there was a show going on, and we'd all get tattooed by Elio for free. I'd make the coffee, we'd all get tatted, have a few beers; it was fun. Later, I started letting Elio tattoo other people here to make a few bucks. I think I even tattooed Roger in my kitchen.

To me, tattooing represents the trilogy of life: you can put your religion, your family, your friends who you wish to rest in peace. You might put something like your football club or favorite team. Later on, the tribal thing came around in America. I don't know what tribe *you* belong to, but if you want to belong to *our* tribe, you put "Agnostic Front" on yourself!

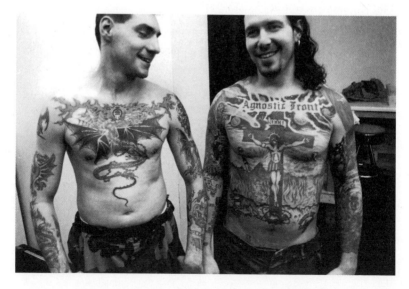

Fast-forward to 1999, I had a few dollars to open up a business. Tattooing had just become legal in New York, so I, along with Jimmy from Murphy's Law, opened up New York Hardcore Tattoos. It was hard getting started, but I got a good deal on the location and decided I could handle it. Jimmy and I would take turns going on tour, but it wasn't run right. We're not businessmen, but people knew who we were, and we had tourists from all over the place who would come in. Basically, we just decided to build the shop and figure it all out later.

There's some important memorabilia in the shop, like Raybeez's boots. He died on September 11, 1997. I had originally brought his boots to the shop that day because I was going to shine them. Every year, I shine his boots on the anniversary of his passing. When I first put my hand in the boot, there was a sponge in there. He used it as the inner sole. I'll never forget that, because I thought it was a mouse or something. Ray had some big feet. We also have a plaque dedicated to him in the shop.

First and foremost, we want people to feel comfortable at the shop. I don't want some rock star type who isn't from our community, with leather pants on, who got sleeved-up overnight giving dirty looks to anybody who wants to come in. Twenty-five years later, New York Hardcore Tattoo is still there.

When I look at somebody and I see their tattoos, I can read it right away. I'm not a fan of these boutique-type tattoos. You can see a boutique tattoo from a mile away. At the end of the day, you're not officially tattooed until you get a BAD tattoo! Then you can say, "Oh shit, I'm tattooed." I mean, it's your business, I don't give a shit, but you can tell by the style of the tattoo, the age of the tattoo. There's no faded glory there. You've got to kind of earn them—and live through them. Also, I've never had any of my tattoos removed.

You never finish getting tattooed. I go years sometimes without getting tattooed. I get distracted. I've only just gotten my hands tattooed. Nowadays, these kids start with their face. The whole culture has changed.

29

Subject

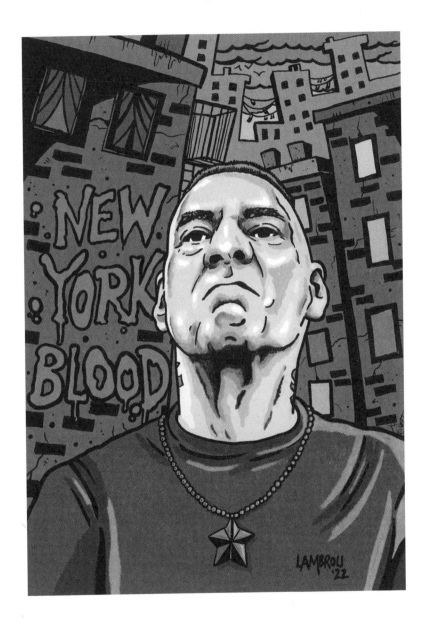

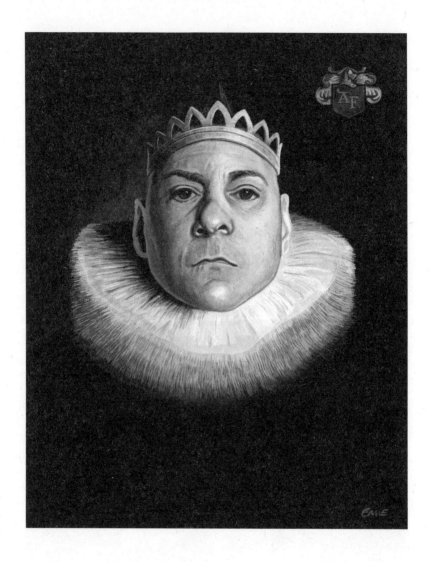

SUBJECT

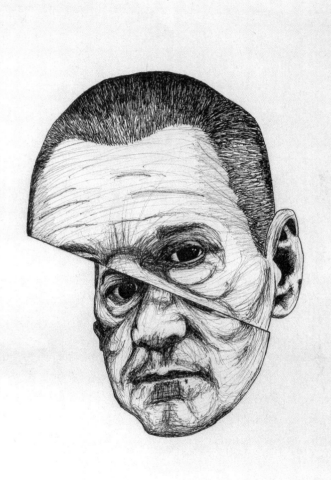

30

Drinking Buddy

I'LL DRINK WITH ANYONE. Wine is more my thing, but I'll drink beer, coffee, whatever. I'm a social guy, so I don't make a big thing out of it. When we're on the road, sometimes people will be looking for Roger, because he handles the band business, but he doesn't drink and usually stays backstage. People would ask for him and I used to tell them that he was by the bar. Then I'd get them to drink with me instead of looking for Roger.

One time I did a Jägermeister promo thing in Germany, and they gave me a belt with a bunch of little Jägermeister bottles on it. I just kept walking around, and people would pick the bottles off my belt and I'd wind up drinking with them.

There are a couple of breweries that have made batches of Agnostic Front beer. Now we have the Jack Daniel's Agnostic Front bottles. I used to make my own beer here at my place. I made Paulie's Bulldog Beer. I could make a soft stout, but not a premium beer. I would usually make a jug, which was a few gallons. I bought a beer kit with the corking machine and some bottles. It takes about a month to ferment. My thinking was that I'd make a batch of beer and then go on tour. Then when I came home from the tour, the beer would be done. When I came home the first time I tried making it, I found that the whole thing exploded all over my house. My feet were sticking to the floor. Next time, I let it ferment in my bathtub in case it exploded again. I learned the hard way. But when it was done, I had Willie help me cork it and put the labels on the bottles. I even brought some to Coney Island High. It was okay, but I finally had my own beer, just like my grandfather had his own wine. Honestly, it's easier just to go buy beer, though.

There are so many people I've gotten drunk with over the years. There was Sean Kilkenny from Dog Eat Dog, who sadly passed away in 2021. Such a great, fun guy and a really good guitar player. A couple years back, Agnostic Front was playing together with Dog Eat Dog at a festival somewhere in Germany. Both bands had finished their sets, and our buses were parked right next to each other. We talked about getting some dinner, and I told Sean that I wanted to shower before we went. We both went back to our buses, and then I headed to the showers they had inside this huge gymnasium. I get in the shower, and Sean comes in with two six-packs of beer and starts pouring beer over the shower divider onto my head. I look out and see it's Sean, so I grab a couple of beers from him and start throwing them at him. Then we realized that some German guy—probably a road manager or bus driver for one of the other bands—was in one of the showers, so we started spraying that guy with beer. We were all cracking up, soaking wet, and just drank the rest of the beers in the shower. Who the fuck drinks beer in the shower? We did!

One time, I was with the guys in the band Discipline from Holland. We were really drunk and they had a fight amongst themselves. The fight spilled into a fucking shop, and the big skinhead guy threw a whole rack of wine onto the floor. The wine went all over the store like a flood. I don't know how we didn't go to jail.

On one of our many trips to Europe, I got a Viking horn from our road manager. It was from a Viking village near the Black Sea. I would drink Viking wine out of it, which was known as mead. I went out one night and got bombed. I came home and was looking for something else to drink. I saw the bottle of mead and the Viking horn and said, "Fuck it, I'm going to do this." I popped open the mead and poured it in the horn. I'm drunk and thinking I'm a Viking now. Then I see all this shit floating in the horn, but I drink from it anyway. I realized later on, I hadn't cured the horn, so it still had the cartilage in it. You're supposed to cure it and put beeswax in it. I got so sick the next day. Mead is the worst to get drunk on because it's so high in sugar. It was literally one of my worst hangovers.

I have a few stories about drinking with the Powerhouse guys in Amsterdam. They were crazy. We were drinking and throwing bottles at people who were in boats in the canal. I can't believe we did that. We should have gone to jail for that too. It's crazy some of the things we got away with. I have a picture from that night with Ernie Cortez. We were dressed as a pizza and a burrito. We were drinking and messing around, arguing about who got to be the burrito. I got a bottle cracked over my head and we just laughed. I didn't get cut or anything. They were kind of thin bottles, but I did have a lump. I couldn't lay my head on a pillow for a week.

I drank with Lemmy at Coney Island High on St. Mark's. He used to hang out there when he was in New York. He was friends with Jimmy G., and we hung out with him there over a few nights. Lemmy just liked to play pinball and drink. He'd either stand by the pinball machine or stand by the bar.

I drank with the Dead Boys and the Dolls at Max's Kansas City....

Here's a good one: Billy Psycho was a good friend. Horrible drummer though. The worst. He used to get so drunk, he would fall off the drum stool when he played. I loved it. One night I was hanging out drinking with Billy and Watford Jon, a.k.a. Jonny Bargy and decided to do half a tab of acid. We started tripping, and were running all around the Lower East Side. Just having fun, laughing, running after people, and doing crazy stuff that I'd probably go to jail for today.

Jonny was drinking Canadian Ace. It was one of the first malt liquors you could buy in a 40 oz. bottle. We were drinking out of the same bottle, and all of a sudden, while Billy was taking a swig, his tooth fell out and dropped into the bottle. We weren't going to waste the beer, so we continued to drink it and made sure we didn't swallow his tooth. We were all tripping and talking shit: "Don't swallow the tooth, I might have to pick it out of your shit. I'm going to have to take you to the bathroom and get it out."

We finished the bottle and were now trying to get the tooth out of it. We're shaking the bottle, but it won't come out. The tooth was stuck to the side of the bottle. I threw the bottle in the street to break it, moved the glass away and picked the tooth out. I put it in my pocket with all my guitar picks. I told him to come to my house and I'd Krazy Glue the tooth back into his head.

So, off we went to buy more beer, and then headed back to my house. I took his tooth and the Krazy Glue and stuck the tooth back in his mouth. I looked at it, but it didn't look right. Turns out, I glued it backwards, and it looked like a snaggletooth. Now I'm trying to yank the tooth back out. It finally comes out and I glue it back in again, this time the right way. I stick it back in and tell him, "Look how beautiful you look! Let me see them pearly whites." We laughed all night at that, still tripping our asses off.

A couple of weeks later, Billy got his head tattooed in my kitchen. I remember hearing the machine going on his skull. He got a big eagle wrapped around the back of his head.

Years later, we covered the Psychos song "Colossal Man" with Madball, which is about Billy Psycho. I could listen to that song over and over again. What a great moment in time.

31

Man of the People

ONE OF THE GREATEST THINGS I get from touring and playing music is meeting people from all over the world. The first time I went to Italy was very cool. I mean, I'm "Vinnie." How Italian is that?! I still felt kinda out of my element though; I still felt very much like an American. Everything is different there: the food, the people, everything. However, a lot of very warm, welcoming communities. To tell you the truth, the food is a little different here and there, but it's not that different from Italian food in New York.

We've toured mostly Northern Italy, and my family is from Southern Italy—around Naples and that area. I tried not to be a gavone while I was there; I didn't want to be too much, if you know what I mean. Actually, there was a time when I was standing in front of the Colosseum in Rome, and this soldier yelled out, "Yo, Vinnie!" He was a friend from

another band we were friendly with. I told the other guys in Agnostic Front the story, and they were like, "Bullshit." I took them there another time while we were touring to introduce them to the soldier, but this time, he wasn't around. Then, out of nowhere, he pops up, and says, "Stigma!" I said, "See, I told you. They even know me at the Roman Colosseum!" But it was great to be there knowing that so much of my family came over from that beautiful country.

I remember one time in Brazil, people came up to me and thanked me for giving them hope. That meant a lot to me. Some of those people were fans, and some were just people that lived there who had heard of us. I mean, I'm just a regular guy. I just walk around with my friends and meet people. People brought me rosary beads, cake, and a few even invited me into their little shacks that they lived in. The best feeling was being told that I inspire them in some way and that they needed people like me. I've done benefits for a lot of people down there and tried to help out local bands, stuff like that.

In Europe, it's similar. We play lots of festivals all over the continent, and we want to do the best we can for the people, no matter what country we're in, or what the economic or political situation is there. The festivals are in these big open fields with a stage, concessions, merchandise, and all that. Early in the day, if I have nothing to do, I walk out into the field to gain perspective from different areas. Like, what does it look like to the people when I'm on stage? Maybe I should come a little more forward so everyone can see me better from the sides. I try to get the visual, because I want to be able to play to someone no matter where they are in the crowd. I want to connect with them the best I can.

I absolutely love touring Europe. People seem to really love and respect Agnostic Front over there. We walk it like we talk it, and it shows to the audiences. We had a show in Hamburg, Germany, once, and our bus was parked over by a lot of homeless people who were hating that our bus was parked near them. I walked out of the bus, and one of the homeless guys flicks a cigarette at me. I decided I was going to take care of this. We had gotten endorsed by some liquor company that gave us all these bottles of liquor. We were never going to finish it all, so I went back on the bus and gathered all the leftover catering along with a couple bottles of liquor, and started handing it out to the homeless people. They loved it, and told us they would watch our bus for us. They were like my bodyguards after that. You have to treat people, whoever they are, like humans. We've always done that, and it comes back to us (positively) all the time.

One time, we were in this fancy, upper-class hotel, and we all decided to go to the steam room. We're Americans, so we all have towels wrapped around us. All the Europeans, they're just walking around the steam room completely naked, everything hanging out. An older woman walks in with her big bush out there for all to see. Then this guy walks in with his huge belly and starts talking to the lady as if it's nothing that they're naked. People in Europe don't care about nudity, and do not think the way we do about it. I'm sure they were wondering why we were all wearing towels. Shit, I wear a towel around me after showering when I'm at home by myself.

In 2022, we played Hellfest along with Deep Purple. The bills on the festivals over there often have these big classic-rock headliners, so it wasn't really that crazy for us to play with them. Our bus was parked at the festival site early in the morning, and I went to get some coffee and eat breakfast at the catering tent. I was all kinds of banged up from the night before. I wind up running into our old bus driver, Jumanji, who was driving Deep Purple's bus. He tells me to come with him because he has the best coffee in the world on his bus. I love our bus drivers. I make friends with them and bring them cake, cookies, coffee, whatever. I try to treat them well, 'cause it's a tough job. They don't really want to sleep because they want to hang out, but I need them sharp while they're driving. They usually need a guy to ride shotgun with them, so they can drive and talk.

Anyway, I was on their bus, and to my surprise, some of the guys in Deep Purple knew who I was. I couldn't believe it! So, I had my cup of coffee and told them I needed to go and was in the bus next door, so they should pop over if they needed anything. Later in the afternoon, I'm getting ready to go onstage. I think there were about eighty thousand people there. Our intro comes on, and suddenly, I get a tap on my shoulder. Someone says, "Go get 'em, Vinnie!" I turned around, and it was some of the fellas from Deep Purple, their roadies, and Jumanji. I run out onstage and I'm pointing and waving to people to make sure they knew that Deep Purple was over there. Thousands of people in the crowd, and I can't stop looking over at Deep Purple as they're cheering me on. That was really cool.

There used to be a music store in the East Village where I always used to have my guitar worked on. The guy there was really cool to me, so sometimes, I'd go in there just to hang out. One time there's this guy in there. I'm talking with him about guitars or whatever, and after a while, he says, "You wanna smoke a joint?" I'm like, "Yeah, okay." We go behind the store in the backyard and smoke the joint. I noticed this guy has a long beard tucked inside his shirt. So I'm thinking, all right, a hippie; I'm all right with this guy. I come to find out afterward from the guy who ran the store, it was Billy Gibbons from ZZ Top. They were a big band already, but this was before the fuzzy guitar video. I had no idea who I was getting high with. Very nice guy, but I was like,

"Who the hell is this hippie? Look at Rip Van Winkle over here!" I don't know if he tucked the beard in because he didn't want to be recognized, or if it was just his thing. Maybe he just didn't want to burn his beard with the lighter.

I got to hang with Kirk Hammett from Metallica once. Agnostic Front played his horror festival out west. We didn't drink together or anything, but he was telling his wife that I was his hero. I was like, "Who, me?!" I made sure to tell him that I was the worst. Nobody in the world knows me compared to that guy. Really, really nice.

One time I was at a Murphy's Law recording session, and (actress) Marisa Tomei came by. She used to hang out sometimes. At first, I didn't realize who she was, but we got to hang out. I was like, "Hey, what's a nice Italian girl like you doin' over here?" She's like, "How you doin' over there?" She talked the way I talked, and I just loved her from the get. Didn't even realize at that moment that she was a big actress. It's before she won Oscars and all that bullshit. Fast-forward a few years, she's in a cab downtown and I hear, "Hey, Vinnie," and it was Marisa. Just a normal girl. Coulda been my cousin.

Sometimes, I'll get coaxed into prank-calling a fan of the band. I like to do prank calls; they're fun. I remember calling this guy, who happened to be a soldier. I called him and said, "Hey, you're not at our fucking show. I'm going to break your fucking legs. You better come to the fucking show. You don't come, I'm going to come get you. Next time I come to your town, you better be there!"

So, I go back to Florida on the next tour, and we had just finished playing our show. I'm hanging out with Corey Graves and Gen from the Genitorturers at this big aftershow party thrown by Vans. Mike Gallo comes up and tells me there's a guy downstairs who wants to talk to me. I told him to hang on because I was hanging out with Corey and Gen, but Mike tells me I have to go. So I excuse myself and go with Mike.

I walk up and there's this fucking giant guy standing there. He looks like he is eight feet tall and he says, "You're Stigma?" I quietly said, "I think I am," and he tells me I crank called him. I'm thinking, "Holy shit, maybe he took it the wrong way." I think it was his wife who put me up to it. He says to me, "You crank called me." I admitted that I called him, and he starts telling me how much it meant to him that I called him. Turns out, he was deployed in Iraq when he got my crank call on his voicemail. He played it to all his soldier buddies, and it brought a lot of

laughs to them. He was hugging me and crying. His wife was crying. I thought I was just being a wiseass and crank calling someone. Before he left, he told me that he enjoyed the show and kept thanking me for the phone call.

Another time, we were in Texas playing this little show. There's a kid there who seemed like he had special needs. I saw him and said hello. He had an AF shirt on, and told me he loved Agnostic Front, so I took him onstage with me. He had the best time of his life. I made him stay near me the whole show. At the end of the night as I'm loading out equipment, the kid's father comes up to me and can't stop thanking me. He told me that his kid had a great time, and it meant a lot to him and his wife. His wife was off to the side crying because she was so happy. It's the little things....

32

Sports Fan

I DIDN'T PLAY A LOT OF SPORTS as a kid outside of the classic street games like stickball, but I do like sports. I'm not a huge hockey fan, but I enjoy Rangers games. I remember watching them in the '70s when Phil Esposito played. Back then, they didn't wear helmets. My buddy (former Madball guitarist) Mitts is a huge hockey super fan. He even knows how to pronounce every Russian player's name.

As far as baseball goes, I am a Yankees guy. The Mets didn't exist when I was a kid. They began in 1962. I remember when the Mets first started, you could buy a quart of Borden's milk, and there would be a Mets ticket you could cut out from the milk container. Before them, in the National League, there was the Brooklyn Dodgers and New York Giants. New York had three baseball teams. What I liked about the Brooklyn Dodgers was that they had that symphonic band at Ebbets Field, which I loved. It was kooky, but I liked it.

I was a big Mickey Mantle fan. Mantle was like *the* New York personality. When Roger Maris came in, he was a quiet country boy, not a New York guy. Yankee fans didn't like him for a long time. I was, and still am, a big Yogi Berra fan. He's still my favorite out of all the baseball people. He even has his own postage stamp. I never went to his museum in Newark, but a friend of mine had the house next door to him in Montclair, New Jersey. He is also a veteran. He was there at Normandy on the beach during D-Day. Everybody loved Yogi Berra. He had a big falling out with the Yankees, and due to that, he wouldn't do Old Timer's Day for a long time. It was all George Steinbrenner's fault. The Boss eventually had to go to Yogi's house and apologize.

I remember Billy Martin during the Yankees' heyday. He was a mess, but he was one of the best baseball guys ever. Billy Martin was hired (and fired) about five times by George Steinbrenner. His number was retired in 1986. He's buried in the same cemetery as Babe Ruth. Their graves are not far from each other.

I do like basketball, and I am a Knicks fan. The last time they won was in 1973. That's a long time. So many New Yorkers have never seen them win in their lifetime. That's why I cheered for the Chicago Cubs when they finally got to the World Series. I wanted to see them win for their fans. That stadium is great. It has such an old school feel to it. I'd love to have an old stadium like that here. I mean, we had old Yankee Stadium and Shea Stadium. Wanna know the difference between Yankee Stadium and Shea Stadium? The bathroom. If you took your kid to the bathroom in old Yankee Stadium, it was just a trough, and your kid is standing next to some strange guy taking a piss. Shea Stadium was a lot more friendly to children.

When I was a kid, I was a Jets fan because of Joe Namath. Who didn't love Broadway Joe?! I remember in the '70s when he did the commercial for Beauty Mist pantyhose, where he had the stockings on. Only Joe Namath could wear a fur coat and stockings and still be a man's man.

Later on, I became a Giants fan, mostly because of Lawrence Taylor. I used to love when he'd throw the towel over his head and crack out, then go back out on the field and kill people. I remember when he (accidently) broke Joe Theismann's leg. You could hear that snap on national TV. It was hard to watch, but they showed the replay over and over again. Lawrence Taylor changed the dynamic of the game of football.

I even liked the Chicago Bears for a minute. They had Mike Ditka and The Fridge. I loved Refrigerator Perry. It was great when they'd throw him in as a running back to carry the ball. Who could tackle that fat fuck?!

Now I'm a huge Pittsburgh Steelers fan. I went to Pittsburgh back in the day with all my friends, and I noticed how football-crazy Pittsburgh is. I never saw so much football paraphernalia and flags hanging out of windows. I mean, every bar, every restaurant, so many homes.... It was crazy.

Their fans are blue-collar types and are true fans.

I like a lot of college basketball teams: Kentucky Wildcats, Duke Blue Devils.... I am a big Seton Hall Pirates and St. John's fan too. Have you ever watched the full days of March Madness? It goes from about noon until two in the morning and continues for days. You really feel the madness. I'm also a fan of Dick Vitale, the commentator. They don't make guys like him anymore.

I'm a little bit of a soccer guy because of Micky Fitz. Of course, West Ham United has a bit of a punk connection with the Cockney Rejects, and that guy from Iron Maiden is a big supporter. I never understood the fighting-at-soccer-games thing in England and Europe, but it's a huge part of their culture. I like rugby too. I'm a South Sydney Rabbitohs fan because my friends are Rabbitohs fans. Great sport!

33

Entertainment Fan

TO BE CLEAR, I THINK OF MYSELF as an entertainer first and foremost, and I have great respect for those who make a living entertaining others, whether they're musicians, actors, or anything else. It takes talent and balls.

Truthfully, I don't think I can make a list of my top ten all-time favorite records. It's too hard, but there'd be everything from Frank Sinatra, The Stranglers, Bob Marley, that Sex Pistols album, The Clash, to Enrico Caruso, Hendrix, The Stimulators.... There are so many great ones.

As far as film and actors, I can say that Clint Eastwood is easily my favorite actor and director. He is a man among men. He is Hollywood, but not really a Hollywood guy. He doesn't have that attitude. He is in his nineties and still making movies.

At the end of the day, I love the classics: *The Good, The Bad and The Ugly, Angel Eyes, The Dirty Dozen*. Some classic actors like Eli Wallach, Lee Van Cleef, Charles Bronson, Audie Murphy, Rory Calhoun, Anthony Quinn, Aldo Ray, and Eddie Albert. I do like Mel Gibson, both as an actor and a director. Frank Sinatra was a good actor too.

Look at a guy like Victor McLaglen. He's a big hunk of a man who was a boxer before he became an actor. When you see this guy and he gives you the eye, you know it. Not like the actors of today. They're not believable, they're too small.

There's a few Japanese actors I like too. I remember a movie called *Red Sun*. It was a western that Charles Bronson was in, and there was a guy in it named Toshirō Mifune. The whole movie is about honor.

Of course, I also like *The Godfather*. I'm a Pacino fan, and like Robert De Niro too. I wish they would've had Robert Duvall in *The Godfather III*. The movie was too much about Sofia Coppola's character. I like the mob films, but especially the older ones such as *Angels with Dirty Faces* and *The Roaring Twenties*. There's a social aspect to it. The soldiers went to fight in World War I, and when they came back, that's how it was. These guys could handle a gun but couldn't get a job. And I love the endings of the old gangster films, like *White Heat*. The one where he gets shot on the steps of the church. Then, he runs up the stairs, comes back down, goes back up, and then he rolls down the steps. The crowd gathers around; you see it from an overhead view, and the cop says, "Hey, does anybody know this guy?" The girl says, "Yeah, he used to be a big shot."

As far as actresses go, I love Maureen O'Hara. I think she was great. I'm a fan of Debra Winger, Hilary Swank, and Meryl Streep. Lucille Ball was great. I don't like flashy actresses.

For TV shows, Who didn't like Telly Savalas in *Kojak*? I watched *Good Times* because I liked the message that every episode would put out, and J.J. was a funny character. I liked *The Twilight Zone, The Honeymooners, The Odd Couple,* and *I Love Lucy….* I think the last TV show that I really watched was *Seinfeld*.

Oh man, I loved cartoons as a kid: *Betty Boop, Popeye, Looney Tunes,* and *The Flintstones*. I was a big *Little Rascals* fan also. On Saturdays there would be four episodes in a row and then you'd watch wrestling at noon.

I also love martial arts movies. Shaw Brothers made *great* martial arts movies. Of course, you can't talk about martial arts movies without mentioning the greatness that is Bruce Lee. You already know how I feel about Bruce Lee.

34

Social Media Holdout

I don't really use any of those social media apps. I only do the internet thing with Agnostic Front and stuff like that. As far as I'm concerned, I'll see you when I get there. I guess I have a book coming out, so just buy the book if you wanna know something about me. That I'll promote, but this, *look at me walking my dog* stuff…c'mon. I guess it's kinda fun, but it's unnecessary. Maybe I'll write "Happy Birthday," or "Merry Christmas," or "Happy Chanukah," or "Happy St. Patrick's Day…." I'm

cool with that, but this *here's what I'm eating* bullshit is not me. I'm too busy. Too busy *doing*. I mean, I'm out there on stage. People know where to find me, even in other parts of the world. The whole itinerary is available. And when I'm back home, I want to just shut it off. I don't need to have this superficial interaction with people, because I get to see them face-to-face all the time. I do this stuff in person, so why do I need to be on social media? Plus, you say the "wrong" thing one day, and you get haters. I ain't got time in my life for that.

I always tell kids, "Go make some friends." I have friends all over that love to be with me. If I need a pair of sneakers, or if I need my guitar fixed, or a ride, or I'm hungry, I have friends. Now with social networking, it is a lot easier to connect with someone, but you aren't necessarily *friends*. In order to make a friend, you have to *be* a friend. When a kid is on Facebook and comes to a show, you finally get to meet them face-to-face. There's already a connection, which is great, so give them a hug, get together, and hang out. Get on the phone and let people hear your voice instead of sitting behind a screen. It's much more fun. Even write a letter.

I can't tell you how many people still have letters I wrote to them. I have people who bring me letters I wrote to them twenty-five years ago. There's a guy who sold merchandise on our last tour. He brought me a letter he saved from about twenty-five or thirty years ago. I couldn't believe it. We reconnected and went to a Knicks game just before COVID hit. Another guy I know, he's still got a Christmas card I wrote to him years ago. I loved to write Christmas cards to people. To think that people from around the world have held onto cards and letters I wrote them after all these years is amazing.

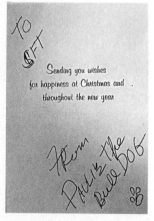

{ 142 }

35

Poet

UNTITLED

I was a Roman soldier 2000 years ago,
and you were my wife.
We were very happy.
We had three children: Damiano, Fabrizio, and my daughter Athena,
who reminds me so much of you.
I died at the battle of Carthage.
They took my sword and my shield…and you cried.

I WROTE THIS A WHILE BACK. It's about feeling like you've lived other lives. Reincarnation, or deja vu. Feeling as though maybe you've lived before.

36

Fitness Enthusiast

I WAS WAY INTO KARATE/MARTIAL ARTS for a while. I meditated and used to be a runner. I was a limber guy and could lift my leg all the way up to my head. I would go to bars and bet some guy that I could do it. I didn't even need to stretch; I was that limber. I would make like I wasn't sure I could do it, and then hustle them for two beers. I got into a little bit of weed meditation for a while, as medicine. I was also into Chinese medicine. I think that I owe my fit lifestyle to practicing martial arts when I was young. It has continued to carry me through my life. I always ate well, and never gained a lot of weight. Instead of eating junk food, I ate Italian food. Not a lot of fat and lots of natural ingredients.

37

The Nose

(A Children's Story)

he year was **1955** when Vincent and Teresa Capuccio welcomed their bouncing bundle of joy, Vincent, to the world. He was a happy baby: always smiling and eager to play with anyone and everyone. As normal a child as normal can be. Because his father was also named Vincent, his parents decided to refer to their newborn simply as Vinnie.

Vinnie was raised in a huge Italian family, with many aunts, uncles, and cousins around to help him along. They would play peek-a-boo with him, tickle him, and do anything they could to make him laugh. All of them loved Vinnie with all their heart. However, each noticed there was something very unique about Vinnie, but no one dared say it out loud.... The child had a very, very, very big nose! A giant schnozzola!

At first they thought Vinnie's nose was adorable, but they became increasingly concerned that as Vinnie got older, the neighborhood kids might tease him about his oversized honker as it grew along with the rest of his face.

Sure enough, as Vinnie entered kindergarten, his family's fears became realized. Kids can be mean sometimes, and many of the children in Vinnie's class zeroed in on his exaggerated snout. It was difficult to ignore. They called him names like **Aardvark** and **Anteater** and **Elephant Boy**. This all made Vinnie very sad and self-conscious.

His family tried their best to cheer him up, but it was difficult. Vinnie really wanted to be accepted by the other boys and girls, but they behaved terribly toward him, with their name-calling and their taunts. They teased him to no end.

This went on for a few years, until one day, Vinnie's favorite aunt brought him a wonderful present. It was a guitar. She'd seen it in the window of a local music shop and thought it would be just the thing to keep Vinnie occupied and take his mind off of all the attention being paid to his nose.

His aunt's instincts were **100** percent right. Vinnie locked himself in his room and taught himself to play the guitar. He even wrote his own songs.

Once Vinnie felt confident enough to share his newfound love of the instrument, the boy asked his parents if they could invite all of his aunts, uncles, and cousins over to their home so that he could perform a concert for them. They were only too happy to do so and gathered everyone into their living room the following afternoon. Vinnie popped out of his room with

a bit of nervousness on his face. He quietly sat in a chair and began to play. His family was equally impressed and thrilled. Once he played his final note, they cheered loudly and hugged and kissed him with great enthusiasm. Vinnie was all smiles.

He returned to his bedroom and had an idea. He thought, If I can play the guitar for the children in my class, maybe they'll react the same way my family did and see me just as one of their friends and not the kid with the big nose.

The next day at school, Vinnie asked his teacher if he could perform for his classmates at lunchtime. The teacher agreed, and once lunch period came, Vinnie sat down and began to strum. His fellow students sat silently with their mouths wide open as young Mr. Capuccio played his first of three original songs. The children began to realize what they had done to him by judging Vinnie solely on his appearance. Some even began to cry with remorse.

As Vinnie completed his final song, his entire class jumped out of their seats and applauded wildly. They became painfully aware of the huge mistake they had made by poking fun at his nose. The group swarmed Vinnie, hugging him and giving him aggressive pats on the back. The boy was overcome with joyful emotion. He realized that his passion for the guitar made his classmates love him, and that he would never be teased for the size of his nose ever again.

38

Brother

(Ode to Roger)

I WAS JUST THINKING THE OTHER DAY: I have no blood siblings, and Roger is my closest family. As close to a brother as I could ever have. I spend more time with him than his wife, kids, cousins, aunts, uncles, or anyone. It's kind of a perfect relationship. When Roger says, "Jump," I ask, "How high?" Because I trust him and know there must be a good reason.

I would never do anything to ruin my relationship with him. I'll never understand bands that blow their careers arguing over a thousand dollars, or even less. Together, we can do better than we could individually. Of course, with Roger, it's not about money. We've been doing this too long. I've loved Roger from the get. He's been my best friend, and now, he's basically my life partner.

We were just touring in Europe, and I said to him, "If I never existed, and there was no Agnostic Front, what do you think you'd be doing right now?" He told me he had no idea. Maybe he would never have met his wife. Maybe he would be a motorcycle mechanic. He might not have gotten so heavily into tattoos. Who knows? So much of what we both are is because of Agnostic Front and our relationship.

More recently, I have worried about his health. He's been through a lot. But he's doing great. He looks good, he's moving around great onstage, he's singing great.... I just want him to be healthy. The other day he had to give himself a shot with an EpiPen. I couldn't watch. I ran away. It's hard for me to see that.

Some days can be rough, though. We finished our (2023) summer tour at the Reload Festival in Germany. It was the last show. This year in Europe it was brutally hot, and it was insanely hot onstage at this thing. We came off stage and I said, "You look like shit." I looked in the

mirror and said, "Man, I look like shit too." We were drained. But neither of us would change what we do for anything. This is our life and our job. We'll do this for as long as we can physically do it.

When I think about it, if I'd never met Roger and we didn't have this band, I probably would've been married with a few kids; I would've had that union job. I'd be retired from the union now, sitting on a couch, bored. Probably have a home in the 'burbs or something like that, instead of living in this apartment. But I think that would've been it. Sent the kids to college and stuff. I don't know. I would have just been one of those neighborhood guys. Maybe dead. My life could have gone a whole different direction.

Thankfully, Roger has this great work ethic, maybe because he's like an old Cuban. Works hard, takes things seriously.... I'm a good go-alonger. I don't give you any trouble. Ask any tour manager, "Who's the best guy you ever tour-managed?" Boom, I'm right here. Hands down. It's like being on vacation when you're with me.

But Roger's story is one of the great American rock'n'roll stories. He comes to America as a kid from communist Cuba. Somehow winds up in Union City, New Jersey; doesn't speak English, abusive step-father; goes to punk clubs in New York City, and who does he meet? *Me*!

Agnostic Front actually tried to go to Cuba to play, but Roger couldn't get in. I still want to go, but not without Roger. I love Cuban food, the cigars, the music, the cars.... I told Rog we should open a car-part business down there, because they have such a hard time getting their hands on parts. They wind up making new parts themselves out of old shit from other model cars. I hope Roger will be allowed back there someday. I really do.

In 1989, when Roger was arrested and later sentenced, my heart just sank into my chest. He was young, and it was a different time in life. Sometimes you make a bad choice. Believe me, I've made plenty of bad choices in my life. Everyone does. The thing is, I feel like he didn't have to do what he did. When all's said and done, you'll never have enough money. Your house will never be big enough. You see somebody else with two ice cream cones, and you've only got a Dixie Cup. You want to get that other ice cream cone, especially if you've got a child. You just want to be the best dad in the world. He was feeling a lot of pressure.

The sentence they gave him was really crazy, too. Originally, he was given four to life. How is that the sentence for what he did? I couldn't make sense of it. When the word "life" is attached, to me, it sounds like you killed twenty people. Even those people are set free sometimes. So many thoughts went through my mind: What's going to happen to his daughter? What's the band gonna do? In the end, he didn't have to serve for that long, but I was really worried about him. Worried for me too.

In the end, Roger and I work great together. We're a great team. I make it easy for him. For instance, the order of the songs for one of our shows: I'm not going to argue with him about what goes where. It's always gonna be, "All right, we'll open up with that, or play that whenever you want to." Or if Roger tells me, "Change of plans, we're going to leave this city tonight instead of in the morning so we can get there early tomorrow," I'll tell him, "Okay, let's go. No hotel tonight. We'll hit the road. We'll drive all night and then we'll get a hotel." No argument here.

To think there are bands out there who actually rob from one another is crazy to me. Guys who let their ego take so much control of them that they think they're (individually) bigger than the band. I can't understand that. You can't operate unless you're a tight unit, not for very long anyway. Roger and I have never had those kinds of problems. We understand what it's all about—and what it takes to keep it together.

If Roger calls me to do something, I just do it. Except he didn't call me just the other day for his little record-release thing at Generation Records only a few blocks from my house, the cocksucker! I guess I was just with him on the road for a few weeks, so maybe he's sick of me. I'm still gonna give him grief though…cocksucker!

39

Contemplator/Reflector

I DO A FEW PUSHUPS, practice a little guitar, go out, and try to have a good time, wherever that may be. Have a few beers, get bombed sometimes, smoke a joint, write a song. I wake up late, throw myself in the shower, cook, clean…. That's what I do now. I got dishpan hands, 'cause that's pretty much all I do: cook and clean.

I do think about the end of Agnostic Front sometimes. COVID made everyone think about life in a different way. The band sat around for a long time not touring, but I practiced, then we rehearsed, and the muscle memory brought it all back.

Obviously, I'm older, but I'm in pretty good shape. To be honest with you, I feel like I'm on top of my game right now. It may have taken over forty years, but I got there. I'm doing well physically. I have my legs under me, and I have my rhythm back.

I actually think the band is doing it better than ever before. We are putting on a better show now. Could be the new guy, Danny, bringing some fresh energy to the band, plus Craig and Mike always bring it. It's like a whole new act. To tell you the truth, this last tour, we were on fire at pretty much every show. We've been killing it, and it's obvious. I felt bad for some of the bands out there with us, but it is what it is. They just need to get out there and hustle more, but all bands have good and bad days. In the end, it's, "When is load-in, where's the backstage, where's the food, what's our set time, let's go!"

I mean, I don't ever look to beat anybody. Of course, I want to do it better than the other bands, I get it, but I don't want to disgrace anyone. I don't feel right if the other bands don't do well. People complain about this and that, but this is what we all signed up for. We're very professional when it comes to what we do. We do the best we can to try to make the whole show go well. Everybody goes home happy. I always cheer for the kids in the other bands. If they do good, good for them. Someone has to replace me one day.

I sing a couple of songs now, which takes a little pressure off of Roger. It breaks the show up into different parts. Plus, I jump into the crowd, and everyone does a circle pit around me. I say to my son, "Any fucking minute, I'm gonna die!"

The last show we played with Social Distortion, we brought Jonny "2 Bags" up to play guitar on "Power" while I sang. We had Chris from Do or Die come up and do a song. He used to roadie for us. I had a girl named Elise come up and play piano. She does "Gotta Go" in a classical arrangement. I had her start off the song and then the band followed. It worked out so well. At the end, we took a picture with Jonny and Elise;

all of us with the crowd. We try to keep it loose and fun, even in front of the big festival crowds. And to think, there was once a time, way back, when Mike Ness and I had a bit of an issue. Thankfully, it's water under the bridge now.

Roger is doing good. He hasn't missed a step at all since his health issues began. He may have a little gray on his chin now, and a few extra pounds on him, but he's been jumping around like normal. This band is still so important to both of us, so whenever he books a tour, I go, and there's never a day off when we're on the road. We're a little crazy still.

Nowadays on tour, I try to wake up as late as I can, but still early enough so that I can get my breakfast and a shower. That's what I do. I hunt around for food. I don't really go visit the other buses like I used to. I don't really run into people unless I see them backstage. If we're on our own, I just fix up my bunk and avoid the heat. I stay close to the nest. I don't really need to go see the Eiffel Tower again, or the castles in Germany over and over. It's cool, but now, I'd rather go to a cafe, or an afternoon lunch to break it up. Maybe a cigar store.

I do love the food in Europe, though. Some of the festivals bring in real chefs to handle the catering. Not every night, but when they do,

it's great. It's different in every city. In Bavaria, my friend Mike from Cafe Central heard we were coming, so he made me bratwurst and mashed potatoes. When we play the Viper Room in Vienna, right across the street, I get my Bolognese. In Denmark, we walked out of the venue, and there was a great restaurant right next door. The guy was a big fan and hooked us up with wine, then the chefs came out and took pictures with us. Whenever I'm somewhere, I try to do as the natives do as much as possible. Eat as the locals eat.

Ultimately, I'm the same person that I've always been. There's almost no difference between me on and off the stage. On the stage, people see a neighborhood guy who they can relate to. I don't consider myself an artist. I'm just a guy who plays in a band. Our band is five guys, a couple of six packs of beer, and some pizza. When we get together and rehearse, our friends still come by: Who wants to smoke a joint? Who wants some pizza? Who wants a beer? That's what I had back in my basement. We'd

all gather down there, order a pie, and do what we did. Agnostic Front has always had this "band of the people" thing. Sadly, people tend to lose that when they try to be too technical, or pay too much attention to being "important." You can be important just by being you and being a good guy. Sure, you want to be able to play well, but you have to entertain first and foremost. Some people cannot do that. I want to be in the moment and connect with other human beings.

I've been to so many incredible places over the course of my life, and had so many unforgettable experiences just being exactly who I am. I never take any of it for granted and try to enjoy every minute, because someday, the curtain is gonna fall on all of us.

Stigma Crossword Puzzle

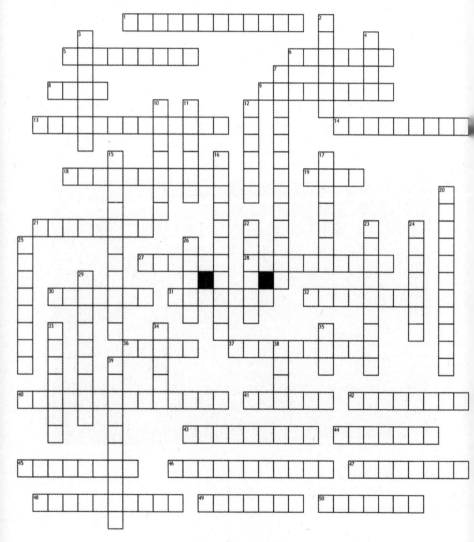

Answer key on page 166.

{ 160 }

ACROSS

1. Director of The Godfathers of Hardcore
5. Fans Form One of These Around Vinnie at Shows These Days
6. Vinnie's Business Venture with Jimmy G., New York Hardcore _____
8. Vinnie's Father Made This in His Basement
9. Vinnie's Wrestling Manager Alias
13. Agnostic Front's Second Album
14. Vinnie's Favorite Rugby Team
18. Straight Ahead, Then AF Bassist _____
19. NYHC Dancing Style
21. Vinnie's Favorite Martial Artist
27. Before It Was CBGB, The Venue Was Called _____ on the Bowery
28. Band Roger Was in Prior to Agnostic Front
30. Record Label Which Released Victim in Pain
31. Short-Lived Original Name for Agnostic Front (Which Vinnie Disliked)
32. The Godfathers of _____
36. Agnostic _____
37. Vinnie's First Band
40. Vinnie's Band Before Agnostic Front
41. Which Guitar Company Makes Vinnie's Signature Instrument
42. Record Label That Released AF's Live at CBGB Album
43. Matt Who Replaced Steve Martin on Guitar
44. Vinnie's Favorite Baseball Team
45. What Subculture Did Agnostic Front Represent Early On
46. Vinnie's All-Time Favorite Guitarist
47. "Do You Want to See the Band or the _____?"
48. Record Label Which Released the Cause for Alarm Album
49. Agnostic Front's 2019 Album
50. Stigma Solo Album _____ Blood

DOWN

2. AF's First Singer John _____
3. Vinnie, Ray Cappo, and Porcell All Have One of These
4. Madball Bassist Beginning in 1992
7. For Which Hardcore Front Man Did Vinnie Become Legal Guardian
10. AF's First Drummer
11. Max's _____ City
12. _____ the Beer Drinking Bulldog
15. Vinnie's Neighborhood
16. Whose Tooth Fell into a Bottle of Beer While Drinking with Vinnie
17. Producer of Victim in Pain
20. Agnostic Front's 7th Album
22. AF's First Music Video Was for This Song
23. Band Originally Responsible for the Song "Crucified"
24. Vinnie's Father and Son's First Name
25. Who Threw a Bottle at Vinnie in the Early '80s
26. United _____
29. One of Vinnie's Favorite NYC Street Games
33. Madball's Second EP, Droppin' Many _____
34. Something's _____ Give
35. _____ Voice
38. Live at _____
39. This Frontman Encouraged Stigma to Go Solo

Image Credits

Steven Messina: pages xvii, xxv, 12, 73, 76, 77, 78, 80,101, 102, 103, 104, 105, 106, 135, 151, 154, 158, 163, insert page 1 top left, insert page 1 top right, insert page 2 top right, insert page 2 bottom, insert page 5 middle left, insert page 5 bottom left, insert page 6, insert page 8 bottom

Rod Orchard: pages 46, 109, 110, 111, 130, 144

Scott Ian: page 33

Craig Silverman: pages 67, 68, 69

Kevin Gill: page 133

Ran.D: pages 28, 30, 45, 53

Jessica Bard: pages 25, 27, 32

Amy Keim: pages 35, 39

Robert Hogg: page 112

Rich Zoeller: page 153

An Maes: pages 60, 152, insert page 1 bottom, insert page 3, insert page 8 top

Louie Beato: page 36

Matt Henderson: page 60, insert page 7 top

Rene Mannich: page 42

Maurice Del-Ciotto: page 159

Howie Abrams: pages 74, 85, 87, 90

BJ Papas: page 47

Photos from the collection of Vinnie Stigma: pages xxiv, 1, 2, 3, 5, 8, 9, 16, 17, 18, 19, 21, 37, 50, 57, 71, 79, 88, 94, 126, 138, 156, 157, insert page 2 top left, insert page 4, insert page 5 top left and right, middle right and bottom right, insert page 7 bottom

"Subject" illustrations by: Casey Lickhalter: pages 122, 123; Alex Rodriguez: 113, 114, 119; Mick Lambrou: 115, 116, 117, 118; Jansen Baracho: 121; Pato Siebenhaar:125; Ernie Parada: 120; and Mike Gallo: 124

"Superhero" illustrations by Ernie Parada

"The Nose (A Children's Story)" illustrations by Bella Kozyreva

Acknowledgments

Vinnie wishes to thank: Vincent III, Kerry Li, Roger, Gallo, Freddy, Howie, Paula, Jimmy G, Jesse Malin, Maggie G, Gary Atlas, WWII corporal John Benante, Cigar Boys, Jacob Hoye and Permuted Press, Ernie Parada, Heather McGrath, special thanks to Steven Messina, Craig Silverman, Danny Lamagna, Kevin Gill and Outlaw Wrestling, Rod Orchard, Casey Lickhalter, Alex Rodriquez, Jansen Baracho, Randall Underwood, Mick Lambrou, Robert Hogg, Scott Ian, Rich Zoeller, An Maes, Jessica Bard, Maurice Del-Ciotto, Matt Henderson, Amy Keim, Rene Mannich, Aleigha Koss, Clayton Ferrell, Pato Siebenhaar, Bella Kozyreva, Louie Beato, Astoria Soundworks, David and Coretex Records, Mark and Generation Records, Paulie the Beer-Drinking Dog and NYHC family worldwide. Sincere apologies if I missed anyone... because I usually do.

Howie thanks: Jacob Hoye, Roger Miret, Mike Gallo, Kevin Gill, Vincent III, Freddy Cricien, Donna McLeer, Heather McGrath, Steven Messina, Cheri Spoerry Gaita, Ernie Parada and most importantly, the inimitable Vinnie Stigma for having me along for this journey, and changing my life with Agnostic Front.

About the Authors

Vinnie Stigma is the founding member and guitarist of the legendary New York hardcore band Agnostic Front. He also performs as a solo artist with Stigma and is the former guitarist of Madball. Vinnie has acted in a number of independent films and has appeared on countless albums as a guest artist.

Howie Abrams is a former music business executive turned author. He co-authored *The ABCs of Metallica* and *Finding Joseph I: An Oral History of H.R. from Bad Brains,* and has written *The Merciless Book of Metal Lists, Misfit Summer Camp: 20 Years on the Road with the Vans Warped Tour, The Blood and the Sweat: The Story of Sick of It All's Koller Brothers, Hip-Hop Alphabet, Hip-Hop Alphabet 2,* and *The ABCs of the Grateful Dead.*

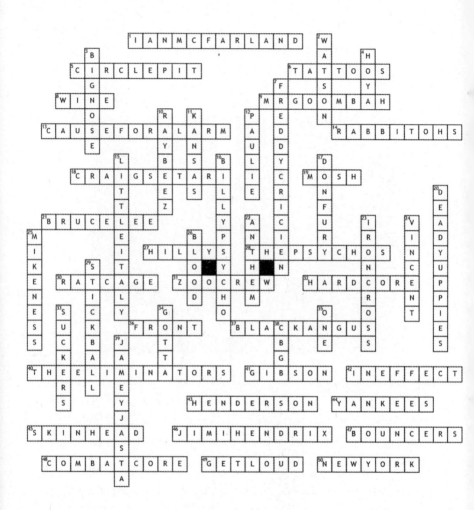